THE MICROGUIDE TO
PROCESS MODELING IN BPMN 2.0
SECOND EDITION

THE MICROGUIDE TO PROCESS MODELING IN BPMN 2.0
SECOND EDITION

TOM DEBEVOISE

AND

RICK GENEVA

ADVANCED COMPONENT RESEARCH, INCORPORATED
LEXINGTON, VIRGINIA
WWW.ACR-PUBS.COM

The MicroGuide to Process Modeling in BPMN 2.0, Second Edition

These books are widely used by corporations and government agencies for training. The publisher offers discounts on this book when ordered in bulk quantities. For more information contact booksurge publications (www.booksurge.com) and query on title or ISBN.

ISBN: 978-1-4635-1135-7

Library of Congress Control Number: 2008902478

Composition and book design by TIPS Technical Publishing, Inc.

Cover design by Jessica Holbrook

Executive Producer: Barbara Anthony.
For marketing, sales and other enquiries contact Barbara.Anthony@acr-pubs.com.

This book is dedicated to all the business analysts who work to improve their firms' processes. In so doing, they improve everyone's experience.

—Tom Debevoise

CONTENTS

FOREWORD TO THE SECOND EDITION

The advent of IT-enabled business process management was first envisioned in "Business Process Management—The Third Wave" by Peter Fingar and Howard Smith in 2002. While initially stated as a language (BPML) to specify process execution, it quickly became, with the introduction of BPMN (business process modeling notation), a model-driven execution approach to defining and enabling business processes. In the nine years following, many companies have created, adopted, or morphed into providers of the software that realized this vision—often called BPMS (business process management software or suites). With the eventual adoption of BPMN 1.0 as an (OMG-endorsed) standard and this standard's evolution to its current BPMN 2.0, the ability to capture and dissolved the nuances of real-world business processes has considerably increased.

However, this is no longer the whole story, if in fact it ever was. For one, BPMN distinguishes itself from most other process modeling approaches in its explicit treatment of events. Defined and digitally captured events can initiate, interrupt, and generally change the pattern of a business processes execution, as they do in real-world process scenarios. To accommodate this need for capturing and correlating simple events into compound or "complex" events, complex event processing (CEP) platforms have emerged as a compliment to BPMS.

Similarly, business rules—comprised of complex combinations of conditions and actions—can now be expressed, stored, and executed by business rules management (BRM) platforms. This line of thinking has further evolved with the introduction of "Decision Management Systems" as described by James Taylor and the more recent writing of von Halle and Goldberg on decision models. While separate books exist on all four topics (process modeling, BPMS, complex event processing, business rules, and decision modeling/management systems), they are often written as if the other topics do not exist.

This book brings together in one authoritative source, with a holistic view, the details of these complimentary concepts. It provides the practical guidance and insights that these authors can uniquely draw upon from their extensive field practice and prior writing in the areas of business process and business rules modeling. More importantly, this book inter-relates the three areas of process, rules/decision models, and event so that the reader is able to see them as both complimentary and synergistic.

While a studious beginner to the arena of business process analysis who plans to use BPMN as their process modeling approach can use this book as an introduction to this fascinating and beneficial look at business processes, this book is perhaps better suited to those with some prior exposure to business process modeling and who wish to know more about the nuances of BPMN (versus other approaches) as well as the complimentary nature of events and rules in capturing an organization's way of doing things.

In a nutshell, this book provides a valuable blueprint for how practitioners can efficiently define business processes, move between the various levels of abstraction needed for summarizing results and more thorough levels of detail needed to ensure successful execution of the resulting models, while taking advantage of the value added from a better consideration of business decision logic and event formulation and processing.

Another aspect that sets this book apart from potential competitors is that it is written in a style that invites cover-to-cover reading. While this can be achieved by overly-simplistic writing, the authors do this in such a way that even professionals will take away a nugget or two of knowledge, while the targeted reader will (after two to four hours of reading) be conversant in the current standards, vocabulary, issues, and opportunities of state-of-the-art BPM and BPMS rules and event processing.

Quite an accomplishment: well done gentlemen!

—Richard Welke
Director, Center for Process Innovation
J. Mack Robinson College of Business, Georgia State University

FOREWORD

Since the introduction of BPMN 1.0 in 2002, many changes have taken place in the modern business environment. We are finally at a point in the business community where Business Process Management (BPM) and Business Process Modeling Notation (BPMN) are widely accepted. In the software business, we often find customers selecting a BPM system as a strategic IT initiative. This is a departure from the previous decade, where BPM systems were sold on their advantages over traditional software development. Often a system was chosen to automate one or two human-centric workflow applications as a tactic for cost savings. Now, many major companies worldwide routinely undertake process improvement initiatives, with a BPM system being a critical part of long-term strategy. BPMN has become the de facto standard for modern process modeling.

Still, changes continue to occur. BPM as a practice is becoming commonplace in the business community, similar to the way Six Sigma and Lean once did. But now (in 2011 and beyond) other concepts such as Complex Event Processing (CEP) and automated decision management are coming of age. Since processes can now be visualized and automated, gaps appear in modern IT systems that cannot be solved with workflow automation. For example, what happens when unexpected situations occur?

Anything that interrupts a planned workflow or business plan can be described as an exception. In today's world, exceptions are the new normal, and we are quickly finding that the optimal, planned way of doing business (the old normal) is exceptionally rare. Solving the problems of exceptions involves a different approach to process modeling which considers the "what if?" and "what else can happen?" as part of the design.

We now live in a chaotic world of constant task switching, social media, the raising of personal expectations, and the accelerated rate of technological change. These factors influence the way we do business. Most attempts to bring order to this chaos using traditional methods have had either limited success or have failed completely.

The old way of handling exceptions is to hire a plethora of managers to make decisions. But today we are constantly asked to do more with less. Consistency of decisions is critical to accomplish organizational goals, which cannot always be achieved when human decision is involved. Furthermore, there is no shortage of information or critical business events. Getting the right information to the right person at the right time is, however, more challenging. Process models that consider business events and exceptions, automated by rules, can help achieve efficiency and restore order to a chaotic, ever-changing business world.

—Rick Geneva

PREFACE

EMERGING PROCESSES
NEW PROCESSES EMERGE

To maintain a sustainable, high quality life in the postmodern world, we face many challenges. The way we do business is dramatically affected by changes in energy prices, global financial markets, unpredictable weather patterns, and other external factors.

To participate in the mandate to build a sustainable world, business must create radically more intelligent, aware, and conscious processes. As borne by the experience of the 2008 credit crash, business processes that ruthlessly exploit a weakness or imbalance in the economy will die and harm the host. These processes ignored or even disguised the wider aspects of risk to the host enterprise and the ecosystem in which they resided. The conclusion is that sustainability is predicated on a balanced relationship between productive and adaptable business processes and risk.

Therefore, intelligence, awareness, and consciousness must be instilled in the next version of process modeling. To attain these qualities, modelers should seek best practices and proven shortcuts to robust solutions. This edition of the Microguide includes methods of modeling with two new critical metaphors: events and decision. It also draws on the author's and industry's discovery of emerging patterns. These patterns, in combination with proficient process modeling, create an efficient path to excellent process design.

Why do we need this? Consider the unprecedented expansion of business processes into home and business, which includes the following:

- Smart grid technology, through which home consumers will control their own pricing and policies with business rules.
- Energy eMobility—with the electric car a completely new source of mobility is arising and customers, OEM, and utilities are participating in new processes known as eMobility.
- Telemedicine, which places appliances in the homes of the elderly and infirm.

Business process modeling not only considers internal factors, but extends into unforeseen areas, often outside the walls of the organization. Modeling these processes cannot be achieved with outdated and incorrect approaches. With this book we hope to update and illuminate a learned modeling approach.

In the first edition, we commented on the benefits of a short, concise book on BPMN. In the second edition, we have extended the length a bit, yet the book you are holding in your hands offers a succinct description of efficient process modeling techniques—the ones that you will need to tackle the problems we mentioned.

THE PROCESS MODELING FRAMEWORK (PMF)

The PMF was introduced in our first edition of the book in 2008. Since this introduction, the structure of PMF has been simplified and made more generic. PMF now works well in a wide range of business areas. PMF has been used to model processes from many different industries including banking, insurance, manufacturing, transportation, and supply chain.

Starting in 2006, PMF was pioneered by Rick Geneva, and (starting in 2008) it was further developed with the help of Tom Debevoise. After the modeling of many processes in BPMN, common patterns emerged. These patterns can be applied universally, to any situation.

THE AUTHORS' MOTIVATIONS

The Authors' Business Model

Tom Debevoise:

As before, we have written this book to provide a service to you, the reader. The service is a rapid understanding of the topic of business process modeling in BPMN. Rick Geneva and I have added even more personal experiences and the experiences of our clients, peers, and students.

For more information on Tom's viewpoints please visit www.tomdebevoise.com.

Rick Geneva:

This book started out as a simple revision to cover the BPMN 2.0 specification. As Tom and I further collaborated, we realized that BPMN is just a means of documenting what the industry is trying to accomplish. There are many books on the market that describe how to create BPMN diagrams. But few books attempt to explain what you should be documenting, and why. Furthermore, we wanted to share our experience on how to create sustainable processes that stand the test of time, crisis, and constant change. And so, this book is not about how to use BPMN—it's about how to expertly model business processes, visualized in BPMN.

For more information on Rick's viewpoints please visit:

www.process-modeling.info

Clearly, BPMN has entered a phase of dominance in business modeling. It is a succinct approach to modeling the merging complexities that we allude to. This book is written to explain how to model processes in BPMN with any methodology.

—Tom Debevoise & Rick Geneva
Spring, 2011

CHAPTER I

INTRODUCTION

INTRODUCTION

With widespread adoption of BPMN, process modeling, if not business process management itself, has entered a new phase. This book covers the BPMN specification, but more importantly, focuses on the paradigm shifts we have observed in the practices of process modeling—for instance, usage patterns that have emerged as best practices and guidelines. These patterns provide syntactic shortcuts to robust solutions.

Process improvement is created with better understanding, communication, and organization—modeling is an important aspect of these. Moreover, modeling translates verbal or tacit understanding into simple metaphors that assist these objectives.

Business process modeling has evolved through new challenges and approaches. These challenges include the participation of social networks, sensors from the Internet of things, and the emerging complexity of a more connected world. New characteristics of the approaches to process modeling include:

- Design of business events, both internal and external, into business processes
- Design of detailed decision modeling into business events, business processes, and coordination of decision outcomes
- Shorter, more succinct process scenarios and business rules
- Incorporation of visibility, in the correct detail, for successive layers of business units, from the most global levels to the local work units
- In addition to the need for a general-level process, recognition of the need for federated, local editions of processes which clarify local processes

1

- Incorporation of monitoring and control for successive layers of business units, from controller roles division levels to execution at the work units

In modern process modeling, process scenarios incorporate a mix of metaphors including decisions and events. A metaphor is a way of reducing the dimensions of the descriptions of a process to a more understandable and visible basis. Metaphors bridge complex concepts and build an understanding of the relationships between them.

The bridging viewpoints are reflected in three manners of thinking: Process, Event, and Decision.

> **Process**—A process can be defined as an organization of activities that happen in a series, relevant to a business's goals and objectives. At a fundamental level, a process diagram represents a single instance of a process. That is, the properly designed purchase order process reflects an instance of a single purchase order, not an organization processing their work load of purchase orders.

> **Event**—From another perspective, a process is actually a connected sequence of events that respond to states, causes, and conditions. In an event-based view, the process is a linkage of the transitions from one processing state to another. The incorporation of external business events is new in modern process modeling. Business events arise from the world outside of the enterprise as opposed to internal events such as key clicks or transactions.

> **Decision**—From yet another viewpoint, all activities and responses to events should be the result of a conscious decision by the organization. The decisions are an assemblage of business rules.

Through any of these approaches, visibility of the process model and the underlying logic increases. A process model is not merely a scenario; it is a scenario that exists within the context of the process, events, and decisions. All these different perspectives are appropriately incorporated in a robust process model.

One objective of this book is to provide you with concrete examples of things you will encounter in your process modeling, matched with these metaphors.

Applied with the proper viewpoint, BPMN is the central tool set necessary for modern process modeling through these metaphors. With BPMN's simple visualizations and problem solving techniques, you will find it easy to create modern, optimized process models.

Visibility and Organizational Alignment

Visibility, organization alignment, and adaptation are critical drivers in the new world of process modeling. Over many years, business analysts and IT have learned to create focused process scenarios, based on outdated, inward looking, and industrial production-based models. In the ultra-connected, fast-paced world, modern processes have shifted from internally focused application integration to a more complex orchestration with the activities of the outside world. This crucial shift, an incorporation of the external conditions, events, and systems, is a natural progression of business models and processes.

Additionally, process visibility is a necessary intangible for high performance management. Visibility is needed in the steps and paths of the process and in the logic of the decisions and events that direct or control those steps and paths. Without visibility, management is left to decipher a deluge of data that can be difficult to relate to a specific process instance.

In this book, we will detail the characteristics and indicators of the powerful usage patterns that are common in all industries. In the next phase of process modeling, we apply these patterns to the problem domain and connect them with organizations motivations. This is described in the culminating chapter on the process modeling framework.

We will also show how to consider outside events and eventually automate decisions with business rules. Finally, we will show how to efficiently model points of data collection for tracking process performance, such as KPI's[1] (Key Performance Indicators) and, metrics.

Business Motivation Model (BMM)

The Object Management Group (OMG)'s Business Motivational Model[2] (BMM) provides a simple road map to connect strategy with business processes, business rules, and business events. It utilizes a set of integrated concepts to define the elements of the business plan. These elements support a variety of approaches for creating and maintaining a BMM. A BMM is particularly strong where business change drives supporting processes.

Figure 1–1 presents a diagram of the BMM. BMM is parameterized in terms of means, ends, influencers, and assessments. It includes reference elements and business vocabulary. The diagram lays out common business vocabulary. These concepts create the BMM, which is a valuable tool for understanding how business processes should be connected.

As its name suggests, motivation is key to the BMM and is deeply tied to the mission of the organization. If an enterprise models a particular approach for its

---

1. KPI: a set of measures that focus on aspects of the organizational performance that is most critical for the current and future success.
2. Object Management Group. Business Maturity Model (BMM) Version 1.1, 2006. http://www.omg.org/spec/BMM/1.1

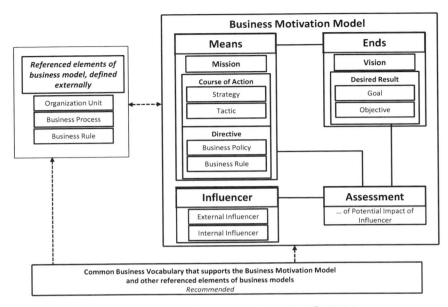

Figure 1–1   *Business processes and business rules in OMG's BMM.*

activities, it should state what results the model will achieve and the business processes and rules that will support it. This is the inception of useful process modeling activities—they address performance holistically.

Business motivation describes both the work practices and information systems; it also describes the enterprise's aspirations, vision, and action plans. It may be imprecise and unformed, but it gives direction and provides inspiration, which filters down to lower conceptual elements in the BMM hierarchy.

The concept diagram shows additional terms and connections. We can chart connections between vision, goals, and objectives, and link mission into strategy for approaching these goals and tactics for achieving the objectives. The term 'ends' corresponds to inspirational concepts like 'vision', 'goal', and 'objective', whereas the term 'means' corresponds to action plans. These can be visualized as a model of ideas formed as a mission, strategy, or tactic. This conjunction of ends and means, being and doing, is the core concept of the model, and in process modeling in BPMN, we create the supporting processes.

The enterprise, however, cannot operate within this model alone and needs several influencers to enable functions and motivate action. Influencers can be inherent strengths or weaknesses. They can also be threats or opportunities. With strengths, weaknesses, opportunities, and threats (SWOT[1]) analysis an organiza-

---

1. SWOT predates the BMM and is credited to Albert Humphrey, a famed business consultant.

tion can determine the impacts of business events, both internal and external, on ends and means. This is the entry point for the business event.

DEFINITIONS

To create a proper process model in BPMN, a grasp of the basic concepts for both business process management and BPMN is needed. Without this, users often create vague or workflow-style diagrams with BPMN, at best. As James Chang[1] has pointed out, traditional or functional work management suffers from a lack of end-to-end focus. In today's BPM industry, the terms such as "business process" and "business rules" have many definitions. We have selected the definitions that you should understand to help you model processes in BPMN.

Business Process Defined

A business process is a sequence of activities that carry out a business goal. There are several viewpoints of what a process actually is. The simplest to understand is the traditional process viewpoint:

> *A business process is an organized, coordinated flow of activities, conducted by participants, acting on and deciding with data, information, and knowledge, to achieve a business goal.*

These definitions arise from a compendium of BPM literature and the business-rules community. It concisely defines:

- The start and end states of process design
- The design choices of BPMN shapes
- The role of business rules
- Knowledge-based control of process relationships with economic conditions

Next, as shown in Figure 1–2, we define the important ideas of the definition:

- An event (shown by a circle shape) is a message, indicator, announcement, or something similar that represents that an instance has happened and has been registered.
- A flow (shown by lines and arrows) is the motion of data from shape to shape. There are two types of flows in a business process—a sequence

---

1. Chang, James. *Business Process Management Systems: Strategy and Implementation.* Auerbach Publications, September 9, 2005.

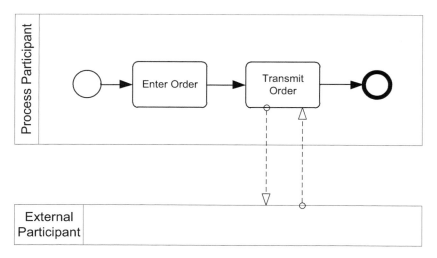

Figure 1–2   *A simple process model in BPMN.*

and a message. Flows can move from event to event, activity to activity, and activity to event.

- An activity (shown by a rounded rectangle) is a task that is performed by a process participant.
- A participant (shown by a horizontal or vertical lane) is any resource that is involved in a business process—be it a person, a group of people, a system, or another process.

The following definitions are not shown on the process model:

- Data consists of structured information owned by a business process. Data can either be structured information or unstructured documents. Business processes can also pass on or transmit and alter unstructured documents.
- Knowledge is information applied to problem-solving. Knowledge adapts the process to conditions beyond the normal operating conditions.
- A business decision is one or more business rules applied to process information.

A process goal is started, for example, when a customer fills out an order form (Goal: Complete Customer Orders). The goal would not be complete until the order is posted to the Enterprise Resource Planning (ERP) system or Customer Relationship Management (CRM) system. There are two types of process goals that are associated with a business process: point-wise goals and steady-state goals. Point-wise goals are the goal of the process with respect to a user, customer, or stakeholder. Steady-state goals are more like continuous metric objectives: quantified and measurable.[1]

In the BMM concept diagram, Figure 1–1, the business process is connected to and supportive of the business model. One aim of this book is to help process modeling teams to illuminate verbal or tacit aspects of a process with sequences of BPMN notation.

These ideas are critical to the proper design of a decision-directed process. Your process analysts will need to identify these within "business conversations." Another goal of this book is to explain how to parse the words. Ideally, the process modeling framework directs your process modeling group's conversations.

Business Process Patterns

Businesses generally fall into a number of categories or patterns, as do their processes. It is important to realize that each process is different. The patterns used are generalizations of common types. If a pattern that otherwise fits your scenario does not match in every detail, do not reject it as a possible basis for your modeling efforts. We describe these six patterns, plus the event and business rule patterns for two reasons:

1. You might recognize your scenario and gain more insight into the needed modeling.
2. They give you some examples of common patterns.

This is by no means an exhaustive list, and every process, event, or rule is different. These are just general types.

The experience of the past few years has shown that most business processes fall into one of these six patterns:

> **Human-Centric**—These processes automate human activities. They create a detailed view of the operational efficiency of human activities. Human-centric systems can include customized order-to cash, personnel on boarding, and applications and claims processing.
>
> **Document Management**—These processes manage the life cycles of documents. They control the versions and maintain a document repository. This often includes branches and chains of a particular document, with several levels of approvals for revisions. You will find these processes in legal systems and heavily regulated fields where there is a requirement for full auditing disclosure.

1. Ould, Martin. *Business Process Management: A Rigorous Approach*, 2005.

System-Integrations—These processes integrate systems and applications to orchestrate their execution. The definition of the process details the validation, movement, and processing of data by different systems. Systems can include the gamut of ERP business areas, internal legacy systems, and trading partner systems.

Opportunity-Specific—These are among the newest types of processes. As conditions and opportunities arise, the process responds appropriately. Events of opportunity are matched with process instances that have the ability to respond to these events. Opportunities are identified through event processing. External events are evaluated, and rules are used to identify the opportunity to which the process responds.

Examples of opportunity-specific processes include integrating mobile phones, advertising, and CRM systems. A retailer can offer a nearby customer (based on GPS data and customer profile) a special discount if they come into the store on a slow day. Another example is the smart power grid that uses a process to efficiently deliver electricity from suppliers to consumers.

Decision-Driven—These processes connect decision points that invoke large sets of business rules. This pattern is used where change is frequent and managers must update the supporting rules and regulations. Examples of decision-driven processes include medical and insurance benefits, certain types of fraud detections, and financial or commodity applications.

Application-Centric—The application-centric process monitors integrations between various applications, and controls the timing cycles and content of transferred data. For example, a process can overlay the CRM, ERP, and supply chain systems. The outcome is a rich view of the organization.

Many applications such as CRM and ERP occur in large enterprises. These systems create a unified view of the customer or accounting information. They have a pre-built database schema and associated application logic. Since every organization is unique, gaps in the business process of the ERP are common. Furthermore, there are integrations with external systems and external organizations. Manual or tacit processes, created by users, bridge the ERP Process. As such, there can be inconsistencies on how data is entered and handled.

Ripping and replacing the ERP with a process-centric system is unrealistic, if not unwarranted. Instead, an application-centric process can be modeled that monitors updates to the flow of data records. For example, a purchase request (PR) is created, approved, released, and a purchase order (PO) is created. These four steps can appear in a straightforward process model. In their original application, dozens of database tables and systems transactions take place.

The resulting process sequence flow can be automated. The automation comes from the applications (CRM, ERP, HR, Accounting, etc) and systems triggering events which are relevant to business transaction. People use the unaltered application, as they ordinarily would, and the business process status is overlaid onto a BPMN process diagram.

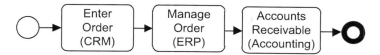

As we mentioned at the start, not every process will fall into one of these patterns and many processes have characteristics of several. They can provide a shortcut to a robust solution for your problem. Moreover, if you need to deploy a process, these patterns will focus the technical choices your team needs to make.

Business Process Management

Business Process Management (BPM) is the identification, understanding, and management of business processes that support a firm's business model. The processes link decisions with people within systems and across organizations. Ideally, the processes support a business model that adapts to changes in economics, customer preferences, and best practices. More often, short-term organizational needs create processes. The scope of these process project portfolios is driven by low performance and disruptions. Processes that cannot adapt to changing economic operating conditions will have a short lifespan.

Business Rules Defined

A business rule is a mediator of information in computer systems for decision-making process participants such as managers, employees, and salespeople. More accurately, and from the viewpoint of the business process:

> *A business rule is an atomic logic step that uses data and knowledge to evaluate part of a proposition about a process decision.*

The business rule "meets" the process through the decision. So, business rules decide with information. When you change the business rule, you change the decision outcome. A solitary business rule can be a policy, a constraint, or a regulatory requirement. Think of a set of business rules as conditions that match data and create conclusions. The rules filter the information needed and decide whether to extend credit to a customer. The business rule is not the decision—it is a logical condition of the decision.

In the BMM in Figure 1–1, the business rule, like the business process, is connected to and supportive of the business model.

Rules evolve in a process to standardize the basis of decisions. At first, people make the decisions based on experience. With time, best practices evolve into an improved set of business rules. The rules automate the most common decisions and promote consistent results. When a decision requires a person's experience, the rule can also decide who in the organization is best qualified to make that decision.

Without explanation, Figure 1–3 presents a process fragment in BPMN with embedded business rules. The objective of the fragment is to assign a customer loyalty discount. The first activity computes the customers total purchases. Next, a gateway assigns a loyalty discount. Each branch of the gateway represents a business rule.

If the business-rules approach was followed, the rules would reside in a "rules repository". The process fragment would appear as shown in Figure 1–4.

Business-Rules Approach Defined

The business-rules approach is a design technique for formalizing an enterprise's critical rules in a form that the manager and technologist understand. The form is simple for business analysts to create and combine with business process approaches. Analysts and subject matter experts gather business rules with the business-rules approach. We will also cover business rules in a later chapter; however, without explanation, the business rules for Figure 1–3 are shown in Figure 1–5.

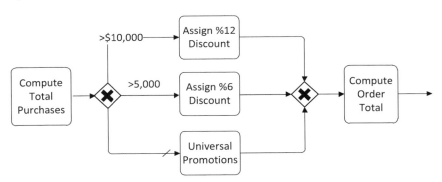

Figure 1–3   *Rules within a process model in BPMN.*

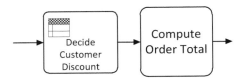

Figure 1–4   *BPMN for re-hosting the business rules in Figure 1–3.*

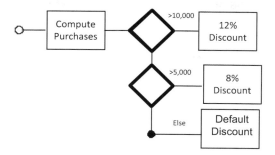

Figure 1–5 *The business rules in Figure 1–3 in decision graph form.*

In the middle phases of process modeling, analysts and subject matter experts discover business rules that support process decisions. Business rules sometimes start with a graphical or textural statement of what a business does with information to decide a proposition. As shown in Figure 1–5, analysts form a graphical representation of the rule from the business language. As with process modeling, the requirements chapter will describe how process modeling teams illuminate verbal or tacit aspects of a decision with a decision graph.

Process Decisions

Business processes use business rules in making decisions, especially in the decision-driven pattern. Decisions are settled with process data evaluated by business-rules management systems. When parsing a graphical or formal statement of a business rule, technical activities define the business objects, logic, translations, or transformations of the rule. The result is a precise definition of the process decision machinery. Since the definition is precise, firms improve process decisions with confidence.

Decision Management Defined

From the perspective of BPM, a decision is a judgment about a business term or idea. The business decision is a determination about a business term or concept. Decision management, then, is the practice of:

1. Identifying decisions within business processes—digitized or otherwise
2. Integrating the decisions into services used by processes or business events
3. Precisely and unambiguously representing and populating a decision model structure with individual business rules

The business rules should be important to, and aligned with, the business during an operating period. The business-rules approach empowers organizations to change business rules to adjust to their needs. Therefore, business processes are more powerful when they are designed with a decision-management approach. We call these "decision-directed processes." Recently, decision management has expanded to incorporate event processing. With decision management, decisions become strategic assets of a firm. As with any asset, their value to the firm is quantifiable and understood.

An advanced form of decision management is known as Enterprise Decision Management (EDM). Taylor and Raden[1] define EDM as "a systematic approach to automating and improving operational business decisions. Enterprise Decision Management aims to increase the precision, consistency, and agility of these decisions while reducing the time taken to decide and the cost of the decision." EDM extends decision management by automating the basis for business rule changes and predicting the outcome of the changes. Advanced EDM architectures can adjust business rules to fine-tune decisions. EDM offers an approach to some of any firm's most challenging problems.

Decision Patterns

Like processes, rule-supported decisions generally fall into a number of categories or patterns. The experience of the past few years has shown that most business decisions fall into one of these four patterns:

> **Computations and Score Carding**—These generally compute one or more metrics. Often, one or more decision tables serve as the final arbitrator. Processes that use these include Credit Risk and Security Targeting.
>
> **Hierarchical or Hierarchical Graphs**—These seek a number of nodes in a large graph of options and factors. Logic can be deeply nested, and the graph can be imperfect. Processes which typically use these include areas of Insurance, Social Benefits, or Entitlements.
>
> **Pattern Matching**—These decisions often apply multivalent or fuzzy logic to data to determine the pattern. Processes that use these are found in the areas of Fraud Detection, Market Abuse, and Security. Pattern matching is used for filtering events.
>
> **Algorithmic Decisions**—These decisions use applied numerical methods, regression techniques, and statistics. Processes that use these are often in the areas of Derivatives, Hedging, and Environmental Modeling.

---

1. Taylor, James and Neil Raden. *Smart Enough Systems: How to Deliver Competitive Advantage by Automating Hidden Decisions.* Prentice Hall, July 9, 2007.

Business Event Defined

In a modern process modeling approach, opportunities, conditions, and factors that events must respond to are handled or managed with business events. Chandy and Schulte[1] define a business event as:

> *A business event is an event that is meaningful for conducting commercial, industrial, and governmental, or trade activities.*

Business events are related to process modeling when the process might be involved or affected. In process modeling in BPMN, we have start, intermediary, non-interrupting, and end events, which correspond directly to a process instance. The event we refer to here is not the various BPMN shapes that we will discuss later; instead we are referring to events that occur both inside and outside the walls of the organization. An event either happened (True) or not at all (False). The event is significant because it might appear in the business process as an external message or channel that one or more processes must consume, activate, and respond.

Complex Event Processing (CEP) is a concept similar to Business Events. CEP deals with vast quantities of events that are aggregated down to a few, more significant business events. Business events are then potentially correlated to a business process instance, or events can start a new process instance. Many business events occur outside the 'bricks and mortar' of the organization, and they have an unpredictable nature. When a predictable pattern is detected in CEP, rules are triggered which potentially match a pattern of a business event.

Business Event Management Defined

The business event management is an emerging design technique for formalizing an enterprise's business events in a comprehensive, concise way. Manager and technologist catalogue the relevant events and determine how to process (filter, correlate, and archive) them. Event processing is a combination of scanning the cloud of events, applying logic to events, and transmitting the events to the appropriate channel. The business-rules approach can be used to develop the logic for event processing.

Business Event Patterns

A business event has three elements: time, data, and a combination of other events. A business event can be explicit and simple, such as an order being placed on a website. A business event can also be implicit and complex, such as when a customer browses ten items from a product category and purchases nothing. The

---

1. Chandy, K. and W. Schulte. *Event Processing: Designing IT Systems for Agile Companies.* McGraw-Hill Osborne Media, September 24, 2009.

enterprise might choose to thank them for shopping and offer them a coupon via email. Now consider unwanted messages that online retailers send customers when they are no longer interested in a product. The element of time is often not considered when these sales incentives are made. Also, for example, when someone purchases a gift for a friend who has had a baby, they might not have children. So, coupons for more baby items are often irrelevant. As in these examples, when we combine several recent events with known data such as customer profile data, we discover a relevant business event pattern.

Like processes and rule-supported decisions, business events generally fall into a number of categories or patterns.

> **Opportunistic**—A pattern of combined events that create another event that starts or alters the course of a business process. For example, the pattern might be within an online store combined with customer profile data. The event triggers a promotional process offering a discount. Then the event triggers another marketing process that displays the value of the promotion. After a few days, the opportunity is irrelevant, and the promotional processes should terminate.

> **Avoidance**—A pattern of events designed for risk management objectives. This pattern is commonly found in the stock market. For example, if the NASDAQ is down 100+ points and prices of a market category are also down, these indicate a 'down market situation'. When a news event occurs, the NASDAQ is in an 'up condition', and a target stocks price starts to deteriorate, an automatic sell is triggered to avoid a massive loss. In 2010, there was an incident in the stock market where "the machines took over", causing the market to plummet substantially. The market automatically recovered shortly. This was a case of automated catastrophe avoidance, later triggering a counteracting opportunistic pattern.

> Other examples of disaster avoidance are found in the power grid, hazardous chemical production plants, and highway traffic management.

> **Notifying**—A pattern of events that trigger a flag or signal that will be observed by a person or a computer system. The events don't directly trigger process action. Instead, the people and systems monitor for event instances. Upon examination, the affected process is manually decided. An example can be found in crime prevention patterns. A criminal offender purchases items that match the profile of prior crimes. Since this might indicate that the offender will commit a crime, the event warrants further monitoring.

> Notifying patterns are more data-centric than the opportunistic or avoidance patterns. Data persistence (storage) is required to correlate

events. In contrast, the opportunistic and avoidance patterns often have significantly shorter time frames.

Deviation—An event model that looks for variation in metrics and key performance indicators (KPI's). For example, the average number of orders per customer is 50. If a customer has more than 70 orders, within a short time frame, then a process alerts management. The customer might be added to a reseller account, or this could be a fraud indicator.

Quantitative—These patterns are the most data intensive event patterns. A large collection of historical trending data is required to provide accurate quantitative analysis. The traditional approach would be to obtain statistics from a periodic report, and this is not adequately agile for the requirements. The event centric approach continuously monitors data. Minimum, maximum, averages, and deviation trends are maintained within fractions of a second of when events occur.

Business Process, Business Rules, and Business Events

As mentioned previously, there are three critical metaphors for BPM 2.0. The newest metaphor in business process modeling is the business event. Table 1–1 lists the important distinctions between the three business metaphors.

Table 1–1   Characteristics of the Three Metaphors

Business Event	Business Process	Business Decision
Unpredictable or random in nature (an external stimulus)	Stateful in nature	Stateless in nature
Monitored by environment and filtered, sorted, and correlated by rules	Sequence of activities conducted by participants	Logic, computations, and business data create actions and outcomes
Based on observation	Sequence of activities, monitoring, and control for participants	Actions, direction, and control for events and processes
Improvements in observations, risk management, agility, and understanding	Improvements in process metrics	More consistent policies, tighter control of business strategies (BMM)
Representation is evolving	Visual BPMN	Visual logic

BPMN CONCEPTS
THE BUILDING BLOCKS OF THE FOUNDATION

Over the years, there have been many evolutions of process modeling prior to the introduction of BPMN. In the early 1900's, the flowchart form of process modeling was developed to represent manufacturing processes. BPMN incorporates a few concepts of flowcharts, XPDL, and other process modeling techniques. Take care not to confuse the symbols and the methods, although they might seem alike.

It is not only the shapes that make the BPMN diagram different from other modeling techniques. BPMN expresses processes in a way that assumes several participants will be involved, and various types of events and decisions will affect process flow. Furthermore, BPMN includes an event handling context that is difficult to represent in any other process modeling approach. In a concise way, BPMN shapes detail the essence of a business process.

Some of these concepts are part of the definitions of business process—an event-activated flow of coordinated activities, conducted by participants, and acting on and deciding with data, information, and knowledge that achieve a goal.

Participant

Designers of the BPMN notation have founded the process on the basis of the participant. A participant is an actor or a person that interacts in a process. The actor includes any human, digital, or virtual resource that is involved in a business process. Participants can include people, systems, machines, other processes, groups of people, and groups of systems.

Processes can also be participants. From a modeling perspective, a process is treated just like another participant. Sometimes, processes interact with each other.

Contract receipting is a good example: the inventory receipt process hands-off to inspectors. This starts the inventory inspection process, which hands-off to material receipting, which starts the invoicing process. These hand-offs conclude with the Account Payable process.

Examples of "People" participants include:

- Inventory receipt clerk inspecting the order
- Customer service rep answering a request
- Employee filling out a requisition
- Patient in a hospital
- Manager approving a requisition
- Technician restoring a disk drive
- Loan officer reviewing an application

System Participants:

- Oracle Financials, JD Edwards, SAP, PeopleSoft
- Database server
- Rules engines
- A telephony queuing switch
- A Web service
- An application server (an EJB or method)
- A custom-built User Interface (UI)
- An enterprise service business, message broker (Sonic, MQ-Series, or Tuxedo queue)

Participants might also be "roles." A role is a logical grouping of people and systems that perform a general work category in the process diagram's context. People and systems can have different roles. Roles rarely mix people and systems. For example, a person enters data and a system receives and processes the data. Although people and systems perform similar work, the role recognizes a division of responsibility within a business process.

Scope Context

A "scope" is a logical container or a placeholder of changing information. By default, all processes have a hierarchy of scope context. At the top is "business process scope," which contains everything in the process. In the scope of the entire top process, a business objective, with well-defined start- and endpoints, exists for the entire process. More refined scopes arise as you break the diagram down into smaller sections with more specific participant (or data) details. Therefore, a logical division of activities and data arises as we add details to our diagram.

Activity

An "activity" is work the participant performs with business processes. Activities are the basic units of process work. In the simplest form, the activity can be atomic (lowest level, indivisible unit of work) or non-atomic (involving many steps). Processes and subprocesses are compound activities. In BPMN, the types of process activities include tasks and subprocesses.

The task is the atomic activity, and since it is atomic, there are no further details. The subprocess is a compound activity that might contain other activities. An activity can be manual, as a human participant completes the activity, or it might be automated by a system participant.

As defined, the activity is a core part of the business process.

Examples of activities include:

- Inspecting material delivery
- Restoring a server
- Completing contract requisition
- Reviewing and approving a requisition
- Reviewing loan application

Flow

"Flow" is the order (and data) in which the activities or process steps are performed. Multiple flows might occur within multiple participant roles. Importantly, the correct BPMN shape defines how flows can be sequenced. Sequences might run sequentially or in parallel. There are two types of flows in a BPMN diagram:

> **Sequence**—Defines the order in which activities are performed for any given process participant. Sequence flow never occurs *between* participants.
>
> **Message**—Defines the flow of information and messages between participants within a process. Messages never occur within the same participant.

Transition

A "transition" describes the hand-off between activities. A transition is more specific than a connection from one process step to the next. Transition means that one activity has stopped and another has started. They are part of the scope of the process, where scope is a snapshot of the process instance data. If each task has a scope, then the scope transitions from one activity to the next, although a transition sequence might simultaneously split into many paths.

Transition never occurs between multiple participants. Imagine a work area with people and workstations for each person's activities (tasks). Participants walk about unaided performing various tasks. As each task is completed, the person transitions to the next task at another workstation. While performing these tasks, participants collect more information and take it to the next workstation, where they may use the information to decide the next task. Here, participants have not communicated with anyone else. Any communication is an interaction, not a transition.

Interaction

Communication between participants takes place with "interactions." Interactions occur between two or more participants in the form of messages. Interactions never occur from one participant back to itself. Note: a flow from one participant back to itself is an activity transition, not an interaction.

Consider the workstation scenario from the transition discussion. Now imagine a work area full of people performing tasks. Participants communicate and ask for help. They might say "I need to know the order number for…" Other participants' tasks may be to complete and forward a document. Other tasks may need an introduction, a handshake, an exchange of information, and a farewell. All these are forms of interactions. As we start to create BPMN diagrams, you will see how this concept applies to your business processes.

Imagine a BPMN diagram of a manual process involving two people communicating. In BPMN, a message is an exchange between those people, including written, verbal, or any other form of communication. In another example, two computer systems communicate in an automated process. A message occurs each time the participants send and receive data and information. An interaction may include a data request and an acknowledgement message.

Process Event

An event is something that happens. A business event is something that happens that is relevant to understanding the organization. The business event is often external to the organization and random. A process event defines a point where the process is either started, stopped, halted, or continued. Events might direct a process from the original flow into an alternate path. Importantly, events define occurring activities "of interest." Normally, participant actions, choices, or activities define or create events. An empty event has undefined criteria, whereas other BPMN event types have a specific trigger condition.

Examples of events include:

- Contract order submitted
- Database unavailable
- Contract requisition completed
- Requisition rejected
- Loan application received

Data

There are only two shapes in BPMN for "data" yet data is a critical part of the business process. Data shapes in BPMN are artifacts, meaning, or an effect of process events occurring. The data is never a cause of process activity occurring. Events trigger activity, resulting in data. Therefore, data models often follow the process model. A well defined process tends to reveal the true relationships between sources of data, and justifies the structure of the data.

All business processes own structured information. This might include business forms, interactions or exchanges between computer systems, documents, activity audit logs, and data from application screens.

Through interactions with others, process participants gather information. For instance:

- An ordering assistant can tell her manager which vendors provide a product.
- A loan processor might receive customer information such as a credit rating.
- The completion of an airline flight contains time in route and fuel consumption information.

Data mostly originates from events. For example, an airplane is cleared for a final approach. This event is added to the flight log (data). The log data is a chronological series of event snapshots. Process activities are initiated based on the status change of the flight now being inbound. Baggage handlers and gate agents spring into action to keep the process moving. Each of these related processes, such as the handling of baggage, generate status, location, timing, and/or cost data.

Each process instance holds a unique collection of data. Each process participant owns information—people provide knowledge, systems have data. Each participant holds their own unique data state. The process maintains an abstract of the status of multiple participants, plus relevant information, in the context of a business objective. The process can contain both temporary state information (what's happening now), as well as permanent records such as the details of a transaction.

The process decisions judge or decide and direct the flow of the process. Business rules direct the decisions and the decision controls the flow and acts on the data. To reach a process decision, business rules evaluate data values. Therefore, business rules use the values from the fields in the structured information.

Processes contribute to the data stream. Decisions also create and manipulate data. For example, a decision may decide what price to apply to an item on a requisition. This is known as a data transformation—data from the process records create other data elements. For example an item's price might be derived from the SCU or item identifier. Figure 1–5 shows a transformation of a customer's spending habits into a discount.

In process models, message flows are used to communicate between participants and other processes. The content of the message is process data. When this data is received by a process, a new copy exists in that process. For example, when I send an email I have a sent item and the recipient receives a new email item. The data contained in the message exists on both ends of the message transmission.

SUMMARY

The definitions and concepts we have covered will prepare you for the material is the later chapters.

Over the last five years, process modeling in BPMN has rapidly evolved. Consistent patterns have emerged and the use of new and powerful metaphors has become standardized.

The over-arching objective of process-modeling BPMN is to understand, institutionalize, improve, and control all the components of a business model. BPMN diagrams accurately and rapidly gather processes and business rules—digitized or otherwise. Without a formal approach, your firm probably gathers rules through legacy, paper-oriented procedures, or a loose tale of data models and "use cases".

The core motivation of process modeling is to gather application requirements from the correct role with the correct method. The outcome is that lower-cost efforts create the process and decisions and then get them right.

A key aim of this book is to describe how process modeling teams illuminate verbal or tacit aspects of processes, events, and decisions with graphical notation. In addition to describing the patterns and metaphors, we intend to empower you to use these tools in your process modeling activities.

With the new era of process modeling, organizations will tackle new and more complex process scenarios. In the final chapters of this book, we will present the process modeling framework (PMF) for incorporating process visibility for successive layers of business units, from division-levels to the work units. The framework will also recognize the need for federated, local editions of processes.

CHAPTER 2

BASICS OF BPMN

In the introduction, we defined BPMN concepts as the key elements of a business process model. This chapter presents BPMN shapes with the aim of modeling a business process with the proper sequence of shapes.

Each BPMN symbol is classified by one of four shape types: rectangle, circle, line, or diamond. The shapes define classes of behaviors. Basic behaviors of the shape types include activities, gateways, events, sequences, and flows. 'Markers' within a shape define its behavior. All shapes reside in a participant's pool.

On one level, a process in BPMN is modeled by ordering these shapes; and order arises from sequences or communications. Shapes sequence with interactions or communicate with messages. With a grasp of the basic shapes and the markers, you can easily create models or read BPMN diagrams.

BASIC BPMN SUBSET—
"OKAY, SO WHAT DO I REALLY NEED TO KNOW?"

The BPMN specification can overwhelm those who are new to process modeling. There is a subset of shapes that occur on most diagrams. This simplifies the diagram and makes the system more accessible to a wider audience. To learn the minimum of BPMN, concentrate on learning these shapes.

Before presenting a detailed definition of the types of events, Figure 2–1 lists the basic pallet of BPMN that every modeler should know by heart.

Many BPMN modeling tools and BPM/workflow automation systems use only the basic BPMN subset. The full BPMN pallet is quite large, and requires a lot of display "real estate". Also, if a tool is focused on ease of use, the full BPMN pallet might provide too many choices to a novice user. For many modeling tools, a right-click or a properties page for a shape will offer more details. This might include messaging options, conditions, escalations, task types, and timing options. Experiment with the modeling tool to see what else is available.

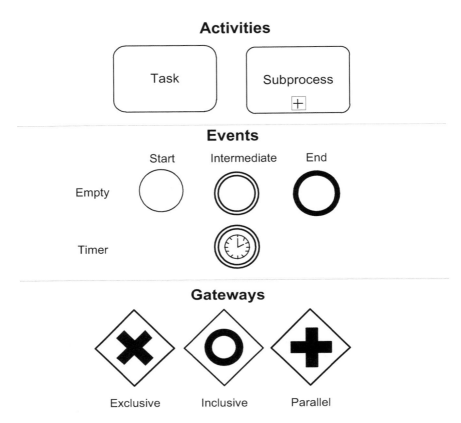

Figure 2–1   *Basic BPMN subset pallet.*

The subset in this figure of shapes is sufficient for most basic workflow processes. To detail various process behaviors, the BPMN specification builds upon these basic shapes. It is recommended that you start building your diagram with the basic subset first before jumping into more complex shapes. For example, an analyst using a message event might consider how the message works. However, an analyst, who draws an empty event might question if it is a message event at all. Chapter 3 will help guide you through this decision.

Before we delve into detailed BPMN, we will define the shape types.

Activities

An activity shape is represented by a rounded box, as exhibited here in Figure 2–2.

It defines where a process step occurs. Activity shapes include three basic types (see Figure 2–3).

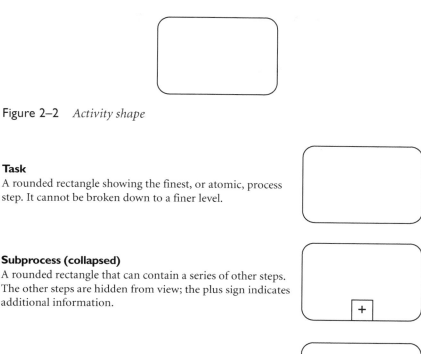

Figure 2–2   *Activity shape*

Task
A rounded rectangle showing the finest, or atomic, process step. It cannot be broken down to a finer level.

Subprocess (collapsed)
A rounded rectangle that can contain a series of other steps. The other steps are hidden from view; the plus sign indicates additional information.

Subprocess (expanded)
A rounded rectangle showing all the subprocess activities (from the collapsed subprocess).

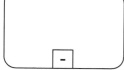

Figure 2–3   *Three basic types of activity shapes.*

Sequence Flow Lines

Sequence lines are denoted by a solid line ending with an arrowhead (as in Figure 2–4). The arrow shows the flow or sequence of a process. This is frequently called *sequence flow* (see Figure 2–5).

Sequence lines define the sequence flow or transition between the logical steps performed by a participant. In the figure below, for instance, the contract is awarded after the bids are evaluated (both by the contract office). Bid Evaluation transitions to Contract Award within the pool contract office.

A transition is conceptualized through the sequence flow line. A sequence flow from one activity or event to the next shows the next as starting—or enabled to start. In the example, "Bid Evaluation" is complete, and "Contract Award" is started.

Figure 2–4   *A sequence line.*

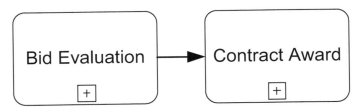

Figure 2–5   *Sequence flow.*

USING THE BASIC SHAPES: PUTTING IT ALL TOGETHER

With this understanding of the basic shapes, you can start building a diagram for a process model. Typical processes, such as supply chain management, serve as the business examples.

Suppose a modeling team is developing core business processes for a contract administration system. Figure 2–6 shows BPMN for a portion of a process's flow of activities.

Figure 2–7 shows a parallel split flow arising in a sequence flow. In parallel branches, process flow might move through any number of activities. Through modeling, analysts record the group's understanding of parallel activities in the process. For instance, they might observe organizational activities and dependencies. Branches might merge, or other branches might finish while other activities might continue to advance through the process.

Implicit Merge

In a simple merge, flow paths are rejoined. Consider a product moving through an inspection process in an inventory process. If there is no defect, the modeler notes that the following activity is "Mark Passed". Otherwise, the defect is identified and reported. In Figure 2–8, the paths that split after Inspect Item are rejoined (merged) at Shelf Item.

This is called an implicit merge because the merge is implied—the tasks merge, rejoining at "Shelf Item", with undefined conditions. The diagram fragment in Figure 2–8 does not specify how the "Mark Passed" task and "Report Defect" merge. The diagram's intentions might initially seem obvious; however, the design can be deceptive.

Figure 2–6   *BPMN for a portion of a process's flow of activities.*

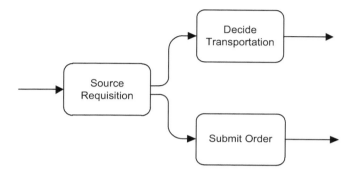

Figure 2–7   *Simple parallel split.*

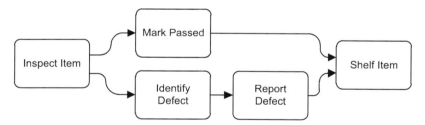

Figure 2–8   *Implicit merge in an inventory process.*

Implicit merges are ambiguous. Since it is implied, one cannot accurately see what happens at the point of the merge (Shelf Item). Perhaps the process will execute or continue uninterruptedly from "Mark Passed" to "Shelf Item". Otherwise, the process might wait until both "Mark Passed" and "Report Defect" tasks complete before continuing to "Shelf Item". For these reasons, and because there is no "flow control", the "Shelf Item" task might execute more than once.

We recommend explicitly specifying the transition from "Inspect Item" to "Identify Defect" with flow controls. This avoids the implicit process merge. Otherwise, the process diagram should describe the merge behavior at the "Shelf Item" point with more shapes. Figure 2–9 shows a choice in defining conditions for the two paths leaving the "Inspect Item" task.

The diamond symbol on a transition path shows the process path when data matches a specified transition condition. The sequence flow line with the slash marks a default path. A condition is a Boolean expression, based on process data

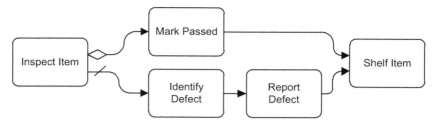

Figure 2–9   *Splitting paths with a condition.*

that control a sequence of activities. For instance, a condition might assess the value of a Pass Inspection flag and follow the transition to "Marked Passed" when the value is "YES." The process follows the default path when the transition condition fails to be true. Whenever conditional paths are specified, use a default path.

Figure 2–9 shows how the process takes a path to either "Mark Passed" or "Identify Defect". A default path clearly states that either path can occur, but not both. By definition, the default path has no condition. The default path indicates the sequence flow that is taken when all other paths do not meet their proscribed conditions.

Gateways

Gateways provide explicit control. A gateway splits or merges paths in a BPMN diagram at a specific point. Gateways direct sequence flows with data, or they specify various path splits. When used as a merge point, a gateway clarifies the implicit merge.

The simple gateway shape is an empty diamond, as shown here.

The simple gateway shape does not specify a behavior. In the BPMN specification, the function of the empty gateway shape is equivalent to the data-based exclusive gateway (described next). Since the data-based exclusive gateway has a clearly-marked explicit behavior, it should be used. A process diagram in Figure 2–10 shows the exclusive gateway with an X 'marker' inside the diamond. For the rest of this book, we will favor the use of more descriptive gateway shapes.

Data-based Exclusive Gateways

The data-based exclusive gateway is a diamond shape with an enclosed X, as shown here.

The data-based gateway shapes are either *exclusive* or *inclusive*. The term data-based means the data in the process selects which transition to take. So, in the data-based "exclusive" gateway, process data defines conditions for the paths leaving the gateway.

The exclusive gateway is used when the process moves along only one path, excluding all other paths. For example, examine Figure 2–10.

Returning to typical business processes, "Truck", "Air Carrier", and "Rail" tasks appear after deciding what form of transportation will be used. The gateway specifies exclusive behavior, the flow takes only one path, and all others are excluded. The sequence flow line to the "Rail task" has a marker indicating the default path. In this example the designer has chosen the "Rail Transportation" as the default, again, always use a default path whenever conditional flows exist.

As mentioned, BPMN includes a data-based inclusive gateway. So, next, it might seem logical to describe this gateway. First, however, an understanding of the concept of parallelism in processes is needed.

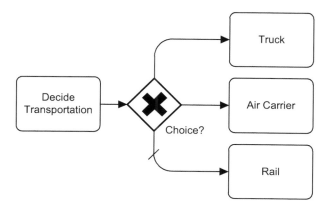

Figure 2–10 *Data-based exclusive gateway.*

Parallel Gateways

A parallel gateway is a diamond shape with an enclosed cross, as shown here.

In the parallel gateway, all paths leaving the gateway are executed (see Figure 2–11). This gateway is used in places where the process unconditionally follows multiple branches. In other words, after the parallel gateway, all the activities occur simultaneously. Parallelism is best when sequential execution is not efficient—for instance, one long-running activity might delay everything else in the process. Here, we use the parallel gateway shape to show multiple activities being performed simultaneously.

There is no default condition when a parallel gateway is used. All paths are always taken and the transition to all paths occurs at the same time.

When deciding whether or not to use a parallel gateway, there are several things to consider:

- Are all tasks always executed? If not, use an exclusive data-based gateway
- Are there any tasks in the sequence that depend on each other? When there is a dependency, use a sequence of tasks rather than parallel
- What is the impact on the subsequent tasks if all paths occur simultaneously?
- In later activities, should the process continue sequentially rather than in parallel? This determines where the parallel sequence flows need to merge before subsequent tasks can begin.

Most often, parallelism is needed for a number of time- or resource-intensive tasks that are unrelated to any other process activity. For instance, external activities such as lab testing or external reviews might take place in parallel, while internal administrative tasks continue.

Explicit Gateway Merge

An explicit gateway merge uses a gateway shape to show the joining of multiple paths. Figure 2–12 shows implicitly merging paths after a gateway shape.

Exactly, what happens at the merge point—the "Release Funds" task? The parallel gateway following the "Terminate Contract" task says that notification of the contractor, contractor administrator, and accounting occurs in parallel. Each

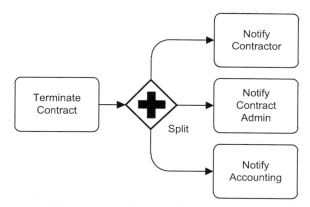

Figure 2–11   *Parallel gateway—all paths will be taken simultaneously.*

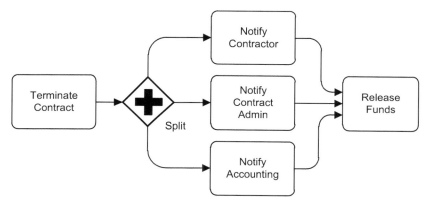

Figure 2–12   *An implicit merge with a parallel split.*

begins at the same time. The notification tasks require different times to complete. One may conclude before the others. So, the diagram does not seem precisely defined at the merge point. Potentially, the Release Funds task could happen three times. Below is an example of why.

After the "Terminate Contract" task, the three notification tasks begin. Suppose "Notify Accounting" completes before "Notify Contract Administration" and transitions to the "Release Funds" task, continuing through the following steps. Meanwhile, the activity at the "Notify Contract Admin" task completes a few hours later. Here, another copy of the "Release Funds" task begins. It continues processing the flow. Finally, the "Notify Contractor" completes, and so forth. Consequently, the "Release Funds" activity has occurred three times. If this is the intent of the process, then the model in Figure 2–13 is correct.

Implicit merges are often obscure and misleading. Figure 2–14 depicts this possible scenario. It also shows what could happen in each path.

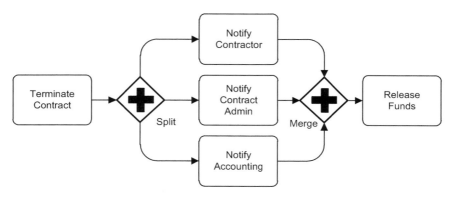

Figure 2–13 *Proper merging of parallel paths.*

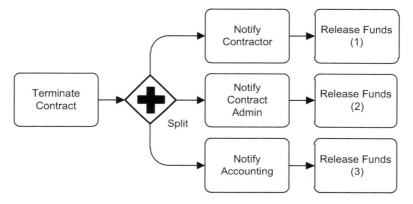

Figure 2–14 *Illustrating the ambiguity of the implicit merge.*

If the "Release Funds" task should not occur three times, then the process might be clearer with a parallel merge. The parallel merge shape is identical to the parallel split. Placement is the only difference between the parallel split and merge.

At the diagram's merge point, before the "Release Funds" task, all paths must complete before continuing. The "Release Funds" task is dependent on the completion of the three notifications; the process will coordinate all paths.

In contrast to a parallel merge shape, the exclusive gateway merges paths, but with different behavior. Figure 2–15 depicts a fragment of a supply chain process.

The data-based exclusive shape can merge activities (here, three notifying activities). The use of the gateway is optional for exclusive paths. Since one path emerges from the gateway after the "Terminate Transport" task, we connect the lines from the notification tasks directly to the "Reverse Freight" task. The exclu-

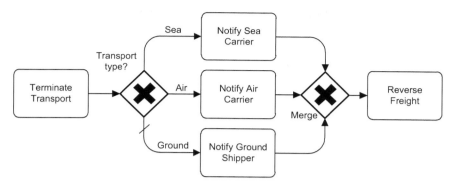

Figure 2–15   *An explicit merge for the exclusive data-based gateway, with a default condition.*

sive data path specifies the merge point, at which the final "Reverse Freight" task is run.

For diagram clarity, the explicit merge point is recommended. A good standard practice is to use an exclusive gateway shape for a merge point if the branch starts with an exclusive gateway. In Figure 2–15, the exclusive gateways for both split and merge document the end of the three paths. As a diagram becomes more detailed, dozens of steps might happen between "Terminate Transport" and "Reverse Freight". As earlier mentioned, the behavior of the implicit merge can be confusing. This might be especially true if a process diagram spans several pages. For example, consider viewing large diagrams on computer screens. You must scroll back and forth to see the entire flow. With merge shapes at the end of paths, the diagram becomes much easier to read. Since parallel and inclusive gateway shapes need a shape to merge flows, the exclusive merge gateway shape is consistent with the rest of the diagram.

Data-Based Inclusive Gateway

The data-based inclusive gateway is a diamond shape with an enclosed circle, as shown here.

Since multiple paths could be taken, this gateway is called inclusive. The gateway evaluates process data against a condition, which is where the term "data-based" comes from. The gateway includes all sequence flows that have a condition that evaluates to "True."

The inclusive gateway shape is a hybrid of the data-based exclusive and parallel gateways. There is a condition for each flow path., and one or more of the conditional paths might be taken.

Figure 2–16 presents a fragment of an order management process. Depending on the order total, various processing steps must be taken.

After the "Receive Order" task, the other paths execute whenever associated conditions are true. If the order amount is over $1000, additional validation occurs to prevent fraud. Additionally, orders over $5000 must be approved by a manager. When none of the conditional paths is taken, the process takes the default path. If the order total is not over $1000, only the standard processing activity occurs.

As with parallel gateways, care should be taken when merging inclusive paths. Consider the process flow after the Standard Processing task if we specify no default path. If no default path is specified and no condition evaluates to true, a deadlock occurs. In a deadlock, the process cannot go past the gateway. It never continues or completes. To avoid a deadlock, if the process needs inclusive gateways, then verify that each has a default path.

As with other gateways, the BPMN specification allows implicit merging for data-based gateways. Again, your design should be unambiguous at the point where sequence flows merge. Also, the use of explicit merging for parallel and implicit gateway shapes is a good best practice. Sometimes a process might perform an optional, added activity, or it might bypass activities under other conditions. An activity is not compulsory on every branch coming from a gateway.

In Figure 2–17, the Receive Order process takes the extra step ("Get Manager Approval") when the order amount is more than $5000. By default, the Get Manager Approval activity is bypassed. With this notation, it is simple to create a default path to bypass the extra step.

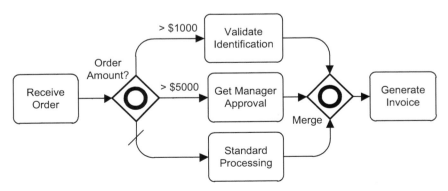

Figure 2–16   *An explicit merge with a data-based inclusive gateway.*

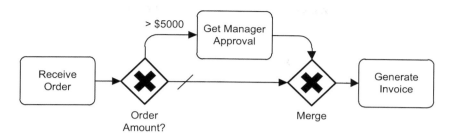

Figure 2–17   *A data-based exclusive gateway controlling an optional step.*

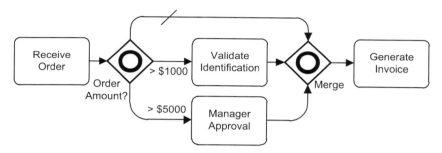

Figure 2–18   *Inclusive gateway with a default bypass path.*

Inclusive gateways might also use transitions without activities. In Figure 2–18, the process's default path bypasses all the conditional paths. Without one or more conditions in the gateway evaluating to "True", the process takes the default path—straight to the merge point—with no additional activities.

Figure 2–18 shows an order management process fragment. The Standard Processing task in Figure 2–17 was replaced with a default path void of activity. As an inclusive gateway, the default path is not taken if any conditional path is true. One or more other tasks (e.g. "Validate Identification", "Manager Approval") can occur in parallel.

Gateway Labels

The transitions entering the gateway in Figures 2–15 through 2–18 are labeled. Document gateway conditions with labels in a question form. For instance, a clear label might be "Selected color?". The sequence flow transitions leaving the gateway should be labeled to answer the question the gateway asks. The answers "red," "blue," and "green" could be possible answers to the question. In Figure 2–18, the answers to the question 'Order Amount?' are covered by the conditions '>$1000' and '>$5000'.

Inclusive/Exclusive Gateway Best Practices

There are a few best practices that should be considered:

- Limit use of the inclusive gateway to situations needing parallel execution. In other situations, try to use multiple exclusive gateways

- Avoid using the inclusive gateway where the conditions are not related, such as document gateways. A gateway should ask only one question— for example, "Selected color?", "Low inventory," and "Order amount more than $5000" can be assigned to separate exclusive gateways.

Ad-hoc Subprocess

Ad-hoc activities must be completed, yet the order in which they are performed is unknown. The ad-hoc subprocess is used for these situations.

Figure 2–19 depicts a vendor evaluation process from a Supplier Relations Management (SRM) process. The four activities must be completed, yet there is no apparent order to the evaluation steps.

Activities inside any subprocess start with the first shape in a sequence flow. When sequence flow is not defined, all the subprocess activities start simultaneously. All activities must stop before the subprocess is complete. Therefore, subprocesses also include an "implicit merge."

An ad-hoc subprocess shows activities that will probably be performed in a sequence, but whose order is not defined. A tilde marker is shown on the subprocess shape when it is ad-hoc. The ad-hoc behavior is different from an implicit split in a subprocess. For example, a grocery list could be like an ad-hoc subprocess. All items on the list are required, but items are added to the cart as they are found in the store—in no particular order and one at a time. In a parallel pattern, all items would be simultaneously added to the cart. Without the ad-hoc marker the subprocess depicts a parallel pattern.

The ad-hoc subprocess simplifies some complex patterns. During the development of a diagram, when the execution order is yet unknown, use the ad-hoc subprocess. A parallel split or a defined sequence flow with gateways describes most processes. In the shopping cart example, however, the ad-hoc subprocess shows the desired pattern with the minimum of shapes.

Events

All events are circular, as in the empty start shape.

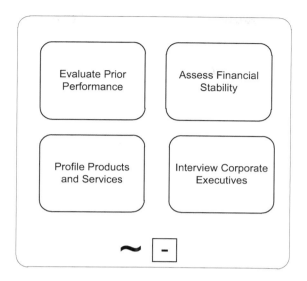

Figure 2–19   *Example of an ad-hoc process.*

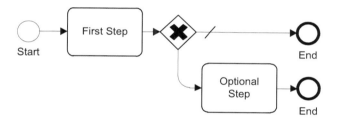

Figure 2–20   *Ending example with a gateway.*

The event shape defines a point of interest within the progress of the process. It can be at the start of a process, the end of a process, or within a process flow (see Figure 2–20).

The event shape is further divided into three major categories, as shown in Tables 2–1.

The BPMN specification allows a process to start with either a task or a gateway. A start event, however, is often a better choice for starting a process diagram. Start events explicitly show how and where the process starts.

Let's begin our discussion of events with the empty start and events shapes. Consider the diagram in Figure 2–20 without the start and end events. With or without the start and end events, the process in the diagram says the same thing. The events define the start and end points for the reader.

Table 2–1   The Event Shape

Start event
This is used at the start of a process. Start event shapes are drawn as a single thin line circle.

Intermediate event
This is used between the start and the end of a process. Intermediate event shapes are drawn as a double thin line circle.

End event
This is used to show where a process flow may end. The shape is drawn with a thick solid line.

There can only be one start event. The end event, however, may be used more than once in a pool. Figure 2–20 shows the usage of more than one end event.

Adding the gateway after the "First Step" task, the optional path is the "Optional Steps" task. Under certain conditions, the process just ends. A process end is an event, not a task. Therefore, the empty end event shape is more suitable for this scenario. Adding the end event simplifies the diagram. Without the end event after the "Optional Step" task, there would be an implicit end. Explicit shapes refine a process design's clarity.

The intermediate empty shape, the double circle, specifies an intriguing point in the diagram or shows a place where the state or status changes. Since the shape is an empty event and behavior is not specified, the description for this shape is uncertain. Consider a business process that has entered a new status. For example, it might transition from a "pending" status to "approved."

The intermediate empty event (as shown in Figure 2–21) documents a point, such as a Key Performance Indicator (KPI), in the diagram. KPI's quantify objec-

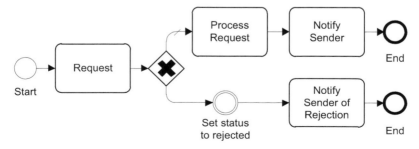

Figure 2–21   *Examples of an intermediate event.*

tives that measure the strategic performance of an organization. When a status changes to "rejected" in the process example, a KPI might be the number of rejected requests. In addition to recording status counts, the process might record more process data at this point. To track this data, a business builds business intelligence (BI) and business activity monitoring (BAM) into the processes.

The rules for the proper use of the intermediate empty event include the following:

1. A transition line must leave and enter an intermediate shape[1]; otherwise, use a start or end event.
2. The intermediate empty event does not show any delay in the process.
3. It does not have any conditions associated with it.
4. It does not imply a point of synchronization.

Terminate Event

The terminate event causes all activities in a process to be immediately ended, and its shape in a BPMN diagram is depicted as shown here.

You can use the terminate event shape to cancel all activities in a process.

In Figure 2–22 the activities "Search for Candidate" and "Negotiate Contract" are enabled to occur in parallel. If contract negotiation fails, it is useless to look for project staff. If the gateway "continue" condition is "No", then the process will terminate. This includes all activity in the Search for Candidates subprocess. Since the Search for Candidates process is ongoing and does not merge with the parallel flow, a terminate event is an excellent option to stop both flows.

A terminate event is not used for process flow that stops normally; rather, it is used for abnormal circumstances. Always use an end event unless there is a specific intention to terminate, such as in the example above.

Participant Pool

The pool shape (shown in Figure 2–23) contains the elements of a process flow performed by the process participant. The pool shape is sometimes called a swimlane, but the terms lane and swimlane can be ambiguous. Be careful not to confuse the term swimlane with a BPMN lane. The term swimlane comes from the UML specification. BPMN does not have a shape called swimlane. Although the

---

1. One exception to the rule is when an intermediate shape is used within an expanded subprocess. This will be discussed later.

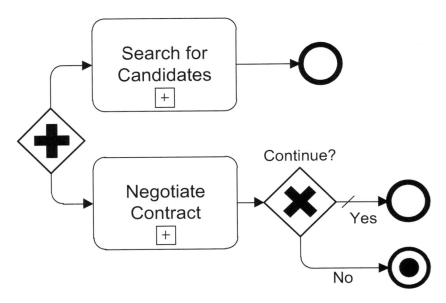

Figure 2–22   *Usage of the terminate event.*

Figure 2–23   *Pool.*

usage of pools and lanes in BPMN are similar to the usage of a swimlane in UML, there are significant differences.

The pool shape represents a participant. As stated in the introduction, a participant is anything involved in the process—a person, a system, or even another process. The pool creates a context for the diagram, referring to a participant. Participants can be specified, such as a manager in HR, or they can be general, such as the entire company.

BPMN allows for a further breakout of pools into logical groupings called lanes. In some cases, this could suggest a role for the participant, such as legal, recruiting, or contract negotiator. But actually, the pool itself is one participant. This is different from the UML swimlane concept where a lane defines a person's role. In BPMN, the role is defined on the pool, and the lane is used to group activity. For example, Figure 2–24 shows the contracting office (a role), with activity groupings in lanes (Contract Negotiation and Staffing Search).

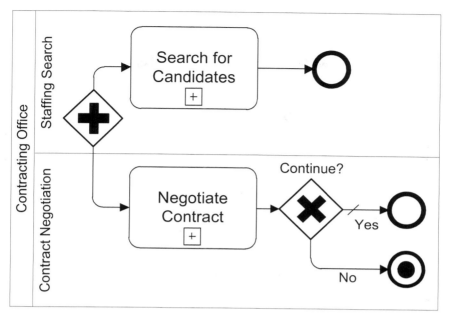

Figure 2–24 *Addition of pool and lanes to the project ramp-up process.*

Usage of lanes is entirely optional. The addition of lanes often adds clarity to the diagram.

To clarify the application of lanes, consider that all activity within a pool is being performed by one participant. The parallel shape indicates that this participant is potentially doing many activities simultaneously. If we want to show that more than one participant is involved, another pool is used. Messaging (covered in the next chapter) is used to coordinate activity between participants.

Another common style of BPMN is to show several participants, such as HR, Accounting, Sales, and Legal, all in one pool, divided by lanes. This is a dated method, the legacy of the flowchart process model. However, there is still justification to use this style today in BPMN. A pool represents a single participant—and a participant can be people, systems, or processes. When the pool represents a process, the participants in that process could logically be grouped into lanes. This is a common approach used in many popular BPM/Workflow automation systems.

SUMMARY

The first part of the chapter presented a basic pallet of shapes that every BPMN designer should know by heart. All but the most complex process scenarios can be modeled with these shapes.

Next, we covered the basics of activities, gateways, and events in BPMN.

In BPMN, a gateway directs the flow of a process. There are three basic gateways: the data-based exclusive gateway, the parallel gateway, and the data-based inclusive gateway.

The data-based exclusive (remember x'clusive) gateway is denoted:

The parallel gateway is denoted:

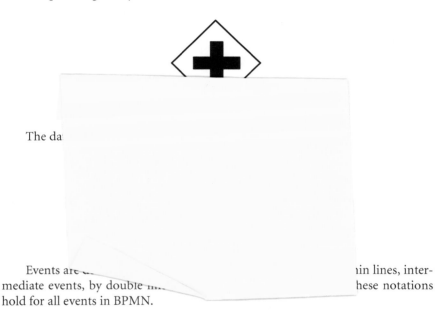

The da:

Events are ...   in lines, intermediate events, by double in...   hese notations hold for all events in BPMN.

CHAPTER 3

BUILDING ON THE BASICS

In Chapter 2, we discussed the basics of BPMN. At first, BPMN seems similar to the flowchart modeling of the past; yet there are distinct differences and improvements. In this chapter we will discuss the advanced features of BPMN, especially events. The Event Driven Architecture (EDA) has evolved the practice of process modeling (see chapter 9), and BPMN is specifically designed to be event-driven and respond to EDA.

Flowcharting assumes linear, fixed process paths, based on anticipated activities. Yet, events in an instance of a true business process proceed in an unpredictable sequence. BPMN allows the process flow to be altered by events. These events include things that happen outside the normal process boundaries, and BPMN can easily model these.

The most common event is the message. For example, in manufacturing, work assignments continue to queue up for a worker, such as for a continuously moving assembly line. However, back-office processes do not follow this inevitable path; and instead, participants are triggered to do things with events. For this reason, messaging is a prominent feature of BPMN.

MESSAGE LINES

Messages are represented with a dashed line, with a circle at the starting end and an arrowhead on the other end. The arrow shows the *message flow* direction.

The concept of interaction, such as participants interacting with each other between pools, is represented by the message line. For instance, when the "Contracting Officer" awards the winning bid to the "Contractor", the message is in the award. Messages are always used between participant pools.

MESSAGE EVENT

There are three basic types of message events—start, intermediate, and end (see Figure 3–1). A fourth type of message, the non-interrupting boundary event, will be covered in the coming chapters. As with the empty start, intermediate, and end shapes, the thin line, double line, and thick line mark where message events can be used within a process flow.

The message shapes display an envelope icon or 'marker' in the center. Each inherits the rules of the corresponding empty start, intermediate, and end event shapes. The start shape event is used at the beginning of a process diagram, and has no sequence flow lines entering it. The end event shape, by definition, cannot have any sequence flow leaving it. The rules are reversed for interactions or message flows. Message start events always receive a message with the line arrowhead pointing at the shape. Message end events can only send messages, with the arrowhead of the message line pointing away from the shape.

THROWING AND CATCHING EVENTS

The term *throwing* means *sending*. The term *catching* means *receiving*. Many event shapes might throw and catch an event. An event is thrown when the event condition is triggered by the shape. An event is caught by any shape designated to handle the corresponding thrown condition. Message events are displayed with a filled icon when sending and with the message (and the unfilled icon) when receiving.

The throwing and catching pattern of filled and empty icons exists with the other event shapes. Filled icons specify an event thrower (sends) and unfilled icons specify an event catcher (receives).

Figure 3–2 shows the use of each message event shape. The BPMN specification allows the intermediate message event to show message lines entering and leaving the shape. However, the intermediate message cannot simultaneously send and receive. Pools represent participants, and a message is between two participants. Therefore, a message communicates between participants. Messages never occur from one shape to another within the same pool. Messages (dashes with open arrows) only occur between pools.

Sometimes process models do not show the interaction details of participants. The focus of the diagram might be with a single participant; however, a model might show the points of interaction. Figure 3–2 shows an example of a collapsed "Pool 2." The pool defines the other participant involvement, without details of the activities. This format is commonly used for an external participant, such as a vendor, supplier, or other third party organization.

Figure 3–3 shows two pools, representing two participants. There is a combination of empty events and message events. First, the empty start event shape in the pool labeled "Contract Officer" shows the start of the process. From the

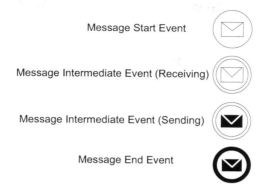

Message Start Event

Message Intermediate Event (Receiving)

Message Intermediate Event (Sending)

Message End Event

Figure 3–1   *The four basic BPMN message events.*

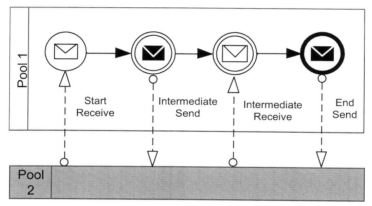

Figure 3–2   *Examples of the four types of messages.*

"Contractor", perspective a process instance starts when a message is received from the Contract Officer. Before this event, the Contractor is not involved in this process.

The message start event starts when a message triggers the event. Then it transitions to the next step ("Change Response") in the process. The message might be an unqualified trigger signal that starts the process, or it may include process data.

Tasks can be a start, intermediate, or end shape. Tasks also can send or receive a message. That is, messages can leave or enter the task boundary. As with the intermediate message event, a task cannot simultaneously send and receive a message. Sending and receiving a message requires two tasks or two intermediate message events.

When a task and an intermediate message event are nearly indistinguishable, which one should be used? As a guideline, if a participant creates a message while working, a task should be used for sending the message. Otherwise, a process responds to an external event and the process models the message as an intermediate message event.

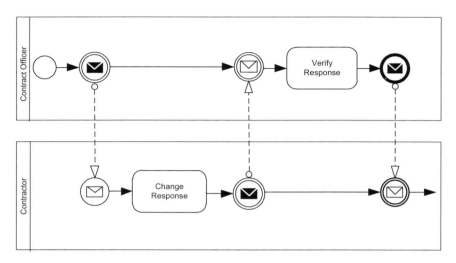

Figure 3–3   *Use of message events between participants. The process is complete when the message in the top pool is sent.*

Consider a busy office environment. A person completes a particular activity and passes a message to someone in another department to perform a step of the business process. To complete the process, this person awaits receipt of information from the other department. However, while waiting for the needed information, this person is busy with other tasks. The business process continues when the information arrives. Using a task to represent a participant awaiting information is allowed in the BPMN specification. However, this implies that the participant has only one job—to wait. In a system-to-system process, this may be an accurate statement, but in a person-to-person process, this is unlikely.

From the perspective of the participant represented by each pool, the intermediate message events indicate the waiting of a process instance until receipts of messages are received from the other participant. The ending for the Contract Officer participant in Figure 3–3 is a sending message end event.

There are important rules for dealing with message events:

- A start message event will never send a message; it only receives.
- An end message event will only send a message; it will never receive.
- An intermediate message event can either send or receive a message, but not both simultaneously.
- When a message is being received in an intermediate event, use the empty envelope (white). When a message is being sent, use the filled envelope (black).

A business process always has one starting point. Processes might start multiple ways, but there is one starting point from the perspective of each participant. For example, a process participant might start process activity by receiving an email, a fax, or a phone call. Regardless of how participants receive information, after receipt of the starting message, they finish their work the same way.

Additionally, processes might wait for information from other participants to continue at multiple intermediate message events. Depending on the data received, there might be multiple outcomes or multiple end events.

When a design requires two or more starting points, separate the process into multiple processes. Otherwise, redraw the process with a single start event followed by a gateway that decides how to proceed. If neither option portrays the process accurately, then use the event-driven exclusive gateway.

SPECIFIC TASK TYPES

The BPMN 2.0 specification adds six subtypes to tasks. First consider the Message Task.

The message task denotes an activity that invokes interaction with another process participant. Earlier, we discussed the use of the message events or an activity that sends a message. It can be difficult to determine if a task or an event should be used. To make the proper choice, decide if the message interaction is synchronous or asynchronous.

Synchronous Messaging

Here the activity requests information from another participant and the message sender must wait for a response before continuing. This is also known as "message blocking". Synchronous messaging is typically depicted in BPMN as a message task.

An example of this is when a courier delivers a package and requires a signature. The package will not be delivered unless there is an acknowledgement that the package was received. Another example is in system to system communication, where as part of a transaction, the remote system sends an acknowledgement.

Asynchronous Messaging

The activity requests information from another participant. However, the message sender is not required to wait for an immediate response. Instead, the sender can do something else, and the recipient will eventually return a response. Asynchronous messaging is typically depicted in BPMN with two message events; one for sending, and the other for receiving.

In Figure 3–4 the Manager first makes a phone call. This is synchronous messaging because it involves an interactive conversation. During the conversation, the manager cannot do anything else. Because the process is blocked from continuing until the task is complete, synchronous messaging is also referred to as blocking.

In the conversation the manager informs the clerk of the task at hand, and to expect a document and instructions. The conversation is complete, so the tasks for both participants are complete. Next the manager sends the document. Between the phone conversation and the receipt of the document, the clerk might be doing something else. It is likely the clerk will react to the receipt of the document according to the priority set by the manager. Similarly, when the document is sent, the manger could be doing something else. But when the manager receives confirmation, his process is now active again (See Table 3–1).

Often, in the early phases of modeling a process, many of the details are unknown, including participants. A good practice is to describe the entire process flow first before attempting to identify who or what performs the tasks. The specific event types defined in BPMN 2.0 are useful for process discovery and documentation. Define what types of activities are involved before identifying who or what completes the activity.

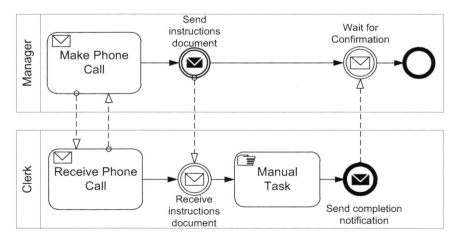

Figure 3–4   *Usage of tasks and events for messaging.*

Table 3–1   Task Shapes

Task Shapes Designated for a Specific Purpose	
Manual Task Task is performed manually, outside the scope of a BPM System (BPMS) or software application such as a CRM or ERP systems.	Manual Task
Human Task Task is performed by a person. This is typically used in a BPM System (BPMS) to differentiate people and system tasks.	Human Task
Message Task Task involves interaction with another participant	Message Task
Service Task Task is performed by a system service.	Service Task
Script Task Represents a software script that runs automatically when the task is activated.	Script Task
Rule Task Represents an activity run by a business rule. Examples include a business rules engine (BRE), software code, or a spreadsheet containing a table of truth.	Rule Task

TIMER EVENTS

The timer event is one of the versatile shapes in BPMN. It expresses a time interval in processing or a wait for a time, or it triggers actions on overdue events, activities, or other processes. The timer events include the start and intermediate, but there is no timer end event. The start and intermediate events appear as shown here.

Start Timer Event **Intermediate Timer Event**

In Figure 3–5, the start timer event shows that a process starts in a given time period. For example, the system runs a report on the last day of each month.

A specified time could be a given day (such as every Friday), the last day of the month, or the first day of each quarter. You could also specify a time such as 2 hours or 3 days.

The intermediate timer event in Figure 3–6 expresses a process wait for a period before continuing. Like the timer start shape, the period may be expressed in an interval's duration, or it may be a calendar date.

The intermediate timer event expresses actions taken when something is not done within a certain period; when we want to take an alternate action such as an escalation path.

In subprocesses, the intermediate event catches a timeout condition. This is shown as a subprocess shape, with the intermediate event attached to the border of the subprocess. Any number of activities takes place in the subprocess. The alternate path starts in Figure 3–7 when the employee does not complete the work within the allotted duration.

SCOPE CANCELLATION AND NON-INTERRUPTING EVENTS

Some modeling scenarios might call for a flow of activities that do not interrupt the sequence flow within the parent subprocess. For example, after a period of inactivity, the process requests a status check without cancelling the current activity. Figure 3–8 introduces a timer event that does not interrupt the subprocess flow.[1]

---

1. Prior to BPMN 2.0, there was only one type of event on a subprocess border. The rules of BPMN 1.2 stated that when an event on the subprocess is triggered, the parent subprocess is discontinued. This includes discontinuing all activity inside the subprocess that triggered the event.

Figure 3–5   *A time-driven report.*

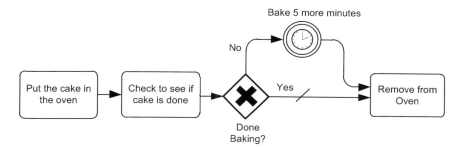

Figure 3–6   *A timer event used as an intermediate event.*

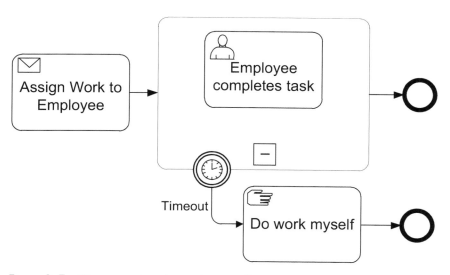

Figure 3–7   *Timer event used as an intermediate event.*

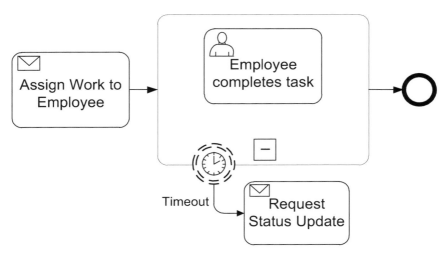

Figure 3–8   *Non-interrupting timer event.*

The timer event in Figure 3–8 is intermediate, but with one variation. The dashed lines on the intermediate event indicate events that do not interrupt the parent subprocess. Non-interrupting events can only be used on a subprocess border.

The timer event is not the only non-interrupting event. As this chapter progresses, we will discuss more event types, along with their respective variations (see Figure 3–9).

Multiple events can be attached to a subprocess's border. As the diagram for the previous example develops, we might determine that a timer is inadequate. For instance, when a message is received from an external source, we might need to explicitly cancel the subprocess.

In Figure 3–10, the other intermediate message event cancels the parent subprocess. The timer does not. The timer is triggered after a period and prompts the manager to check the status of the employee's activity. If the cancellation message is received, the employee's activity is discontinued. Since the employee task was delegated, a notification is sent, informing the employee to stop working on this process instane.

Figure 3–9   *Non-interrupting intermediate timer and message events.*

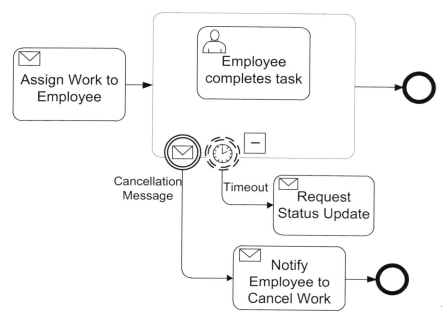

Figure 3–10 *Multiple events on the subprocess border.*

CONDITION EVENTS

The condition event is a bit more sophisticated than the timer and message events. Timers are triggered by time, and messages are triggered when a participant sends a message. A condition event is somewhat more automated and requires an active participant to trigger the condition. For this reason, condition events are typically only used in processes that have a computer system that constantly monitors conditions.

The condition event comes in three varieties: start, intermediate, and intermediate non-interrupting. Figure 3–11 shows an example of the condition start event in use.

It is possible to use the condition event in human-centric processes, but its purpose is often misunderstood. Consider placing a condition event on the activity border when the activity has not completed, and a condition is discovered that should interrupt (Figure 3–12).

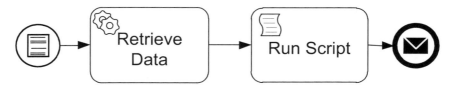

Figure 3–11   *Condition start event triggers an automated process.*

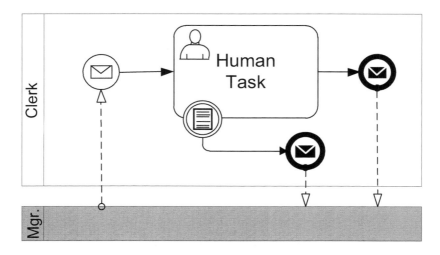

Figure 3–12   *Condition event interrupting a human task.*

If the activity has completed and then later evaluated, the gateway after the activity is more appropriate (Figure 3–13). Take care not to confuse the two use cases. To avoid diagram misinterpretation, use the gateway where appropriate

Without driving data or triggering events, condition events do not arise. Also, a participant must subsequently evaluate the condition. In Figure 3–12, the Clerk participant is responsible for evaluating the condition. In Figure 3–13, a system facility likely monitors activity and triggers the start.

Alternately, the condition event can suggest a hidden or off-diagram participant. Consider Figure 3–12. If the participant were a person, how does the participant receive the data and events to evaluate the condition? This point is not evident by evaluating the diagram. Therefore, in some cases, one should use another event shape instead—such as the signal event.

SIGNAL EVENT

Signal events are depicted by triangles inside circles. There are five types of signal events and corresponding symbols, as shown in Figure 3–14.

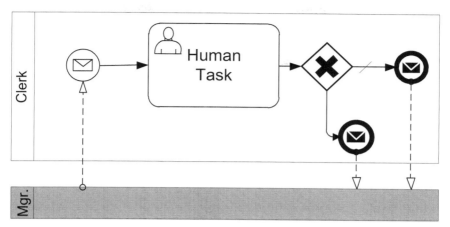

Figure 3–13 *Usage of gateway to determine condition.*

Figure 3–14 *Five types of signal events.*

Ordinary message shapes send a message from one participant to another, yet the process might need to send messages to a group of listening participants. The receiving group might even be uncertain. Thus, the signal pattern is a like a radio broadcast. The signal message continuously broadcasts, and those who want to listen to the broadcast tune in or subscribe.

The signal event can broadcast to all processes simultaneously. The signal intermediate (throwing) and signal end shapes denote this broadcast. The signal start and signal intermediate (catching) events allow an activity to receive a broadcast.

Signal events can also be used for synchronization between parallel branches. In Figure 3–15, activities A1 and B1 begin at the same time. However, B2 cannot begin before A1 is complete. Messages cannot be sent to the same participant in the same pool. Since all participants can potentially receive signals, they can be used in the same pool.

A process might make another broadcast after A2 in Figure 3–15. The signal after B1 could receive either signal from the A branch. Again, the process could be stopped because B1 might take longer to complete than A1 and A2 combined. The addition of the parallel split and merge in Figure 3–16 ensures that A1, B1, and A2, B2 are kept in synch.

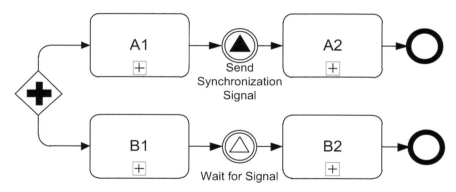

Figure 3–15   *Use of signals for synchronization.*

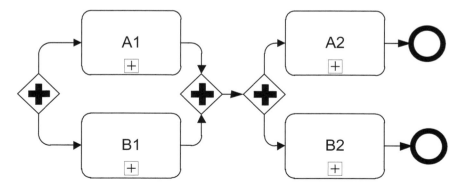

Figure 3–16   *Using parallel merge instead of signals.*

Figure 3–17 shows a busy intersection from the perspective of three partici-pants—a northbound driver, a westbound driver, and the traffic light that helps the two drivers avoid a collision. Drivers entering the intersection determine whether or not to proceed based on the color of the traffic light. The driver

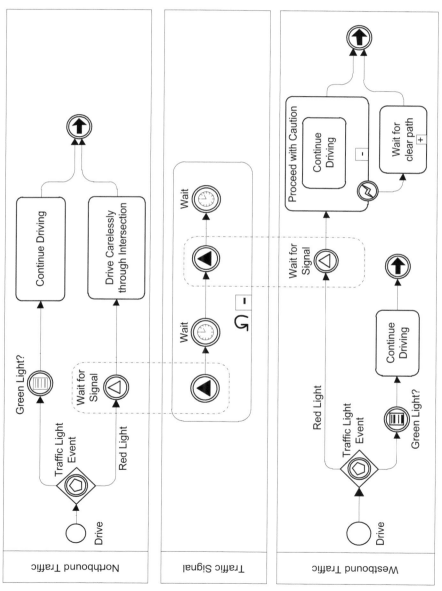

Figure 3–17   *Traffic light diagram using the signal event shapes.*

observes the state and decides. Since the traffic light occurs during normal driving, the traffic signal light is a driver's signal event. The stopped driver proceeds through the intersection if there is a green signal. From the perspective of the traffic light, a green signal signifies send to traffic waiting at a red light.

Without participants, there is no explicit message interaction. Instead of using interaction lines, Figure 3–17 uses the group shape to clarify the relationship between the signal throw and catch events. The usage of the group shape is not mandatory—it just makes the diagram easier to read.

Figure 3–17 illustrates what happens after the signal change. The northbound driver is reckless and hits the accelerator pedal. The westbound driver is more cautious and watches for crossing traffic even though the traffic light signals green. When a speeding driver crosses with indifference to the red signal, an error handling subprocess is managed with this exception condition.

This is an example of how easy it is to represent a complex interaction using just a few BPMN shapes. In fact, if we wrote the whole scenario in words, there would probably be three or four pages. This little diagram shows the perspective of three participants, what they do, and how each action relates to the other participants.

The process in Figure 3–17 contrasts the condition and signal events. In the event gateway, in the condition event shape, participants actively monitor for a condition. There is no guarantee that a signal light will be encountered while driving (the condition). The default event is the green condition, where the criterion is that the signal is recognized, observed, relevant to the driver's lane, and currently green. Otherwise the driver waits for a red signal to turn green (a broadcast).

With the signal event shape, participants observe a broadcast message. The driver subscribes to the signal event and waits for it. The signal event is received by anyone within view of the traffic light (the subscribers). The signal is used in this case because there is already a potential participant. In contrast, the condition event is used when it is not known if a related process exists or not. This is because the act of locating a traffic signal and responding to its current state is fairly complex. It requires a driver to pay attention to many objects as he drives down the road. If the traffic signal were instead an ambulance siren, a signal would be a better choice. With complex criteria for event recognition, a condition should be used instead of a signal.

Event Type Comparison

- Messages are used for point-to-point communication between participants when it is desired to show where interactions exist. Guaranteed message receipt is desired.

- Signals are used for communications where a relevant participant might, or might not exist. The signal sender is not necessarily aware of any specific recipients. Signals are typically used to notify of changing data or processing states to any participant that is interested. Message receipt confirmation is not desired because it would generate too much overhead.

- Conditions are used to detect a possible combination of criteria from multiple sources. A participant is responsible for detecting its own condition criteria because no notification of changing criteria exists.

- Timers are used to trigger events, based on a period of time. These timing events can cause a process to delay, or they can cause an alternate flow after a time period expires.

SUMMARY

We covered the basics of messages and several useful event types in BPMN. Modelers can develop fairly complete processes with the information in this (and the previous) chapter.

We covered six additional tasks that are denoted with special markers. These were:

1. Manual Task (Hand Marker): a manual activity, outside the scope of a BPM System (BPMS)
2. Human Task (Person Marker): a task performed by a person; used to differentiate people and system tasks
3. Message Task (Envelope Marker): a task that involves interaction with another participant
4. Service Task (Gear Marker): a task is performed by a system service
5. Script Task (Script Marker): a software script that runs automatically
6. Rule Task (Page Marker): an activity run by a business rule

Then, we covered timer events and introduced the non-interrupting timer event. We also discussed events that are attached to the boundaries of subprocesses.

Finally, we described the signal event.

In the next chapter, we complete the modeling skill set by covering loops and other forms of multiplicity.

CHAPTER 4

ITERATIONS AND MULTIPLICITY

In the first two BPMN chapters, we developed a basic set of BPMN shapes that can be used to model a business process. As our focus dives into the details of a process, models will need the ability to loop—that is, to loop through records, time, and conditions.

LOOPING ACTIVITY

An activity that repeats for multiple iterations is called a looping activity. Looping activities can be either a task or a subprocess. The marker for the looping task or subprocess is a pointed arc.

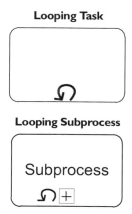

Looping Task

Looping Subprocess

Subprocess

The looping task is a basic activity, performed repeatedly—for instance, a wheel turns. More often, looping activities are subprocesses. Since it is a compound, multi-step activity, a looping subprocess can model a manufacturing assembly line. When the loop ends, the activity is completed, and the process continues to the next activity.

The loop is dependent on a condition—for example, "Continue looping until the document is approved or rejected" (see Figure 4–1). There is nothing that explicitly shows the stop-loop condition. For this reason, a text annotation might be used to describe the loop stopping condition. Annotations will be covered in Chapter 6.

Multiple-Instance Subprocess

Another looping activity type is the multiple-instance subprocess. It completes in a predetermined number of iterations, however, the looping subprocess might denote an indeterminate continuation. If the condition never arrives, the cycles would execute indefinitely. It has two varieties: serial and parallel. The marker for the multiple-instance subprocess is a series of three lines. When the lines are horizontal, the activity is executed in serial, similar to the looping activity. When the lines are vertical, the activity is executed in parallel with all other activities.

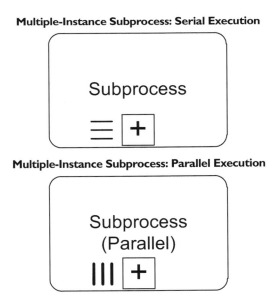

Multiple-Instance Subprocess: Serial Execution

Multiple-Instance Subprocess: Parallel Execution

The multiple-instance activity indicates that something will be done a fixed number of times. For example, a multiple-instance activity could be used for a committee process with ten members where each must vote.

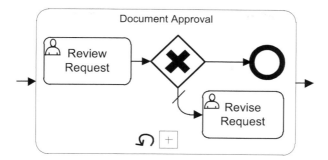

Figure 4–1   *Looping subprocess (expanded).*

The condition for the multiple-instance subprocess might be a fixed amount such as "5," or it might be assigned from the instance's process data—for example, "For each ordered item, add the item's price to the total."

The parallel version of the multiple-instance subprocess is used when all activities should be completed in parallel. The voting process that includes ten committee members is an excellent example of a parallel, multiple-instance activity. Figure 4–2 shows an example of the parallel multiple-instance simultaneously sending and receiving votes from each person from a group of people.

When concurrent execution is faster or more efficient among multiple participants, parallelism can optimize a process. Parallel activity is possible with only one participant. This would imply that all tasks are enabled, but not necessarily executed, in parallel.

Scenarios such as iterating through a stack of documents might call for a serial multiple-instance subprocess. For example, a participant receives five documents that must be signed. The documents can only be signed one at a time (sequentially), and must be kept in order. Therefore, this would impose serial execution. The discerning factor is whether or not a sequence is needed for iteration. Figure 4–2 shows votes being tallied with a serial multiple-instance subprocess. After all votes have been received, a single participant will count the votes—once for each vote received.

For more technical processes, the serial multiple-instance activity denotes a "for-each" loop. Consider the requirement: "for each customer in the southeast, send a promotional email". When the number of customers in the criteria is fixed, use the serial multiple-instance subprocess—instead of the looping subprocess. In contrast, the looping subprocess is more likely a "do-while" or "do-until" loop type, which typically lack a predetermined iteration count. In an approval process, for example, we continue to ask for revisions until the item is either approved or rejected (do-until).

When the multiplicity lines are vertical, all iterations of the activity are enabled to execute in parallel. Parallel execution usually involves multiple participants, although they might not be explicitly shown.

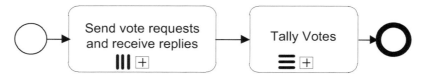

Figure 4–2   *A contrast of serial and parallel multiple instances.*

Looping Styles Contrasted

There are many ways to illustrate looping processes in BPMN. The most common is called "upstream flow". Here the flow routes back (upstream) or to a previously executed activity. Figure 4–3 shows an example of upstream flow. This style of modeling is typically used with multiple lanes inside a single pool.

Often, a looping subprocess is a better choice than the "upstream flow" because it shows a repeating behavior instead of a redo. There are advantages and disadvantages to using the upstream flow method of looping (Figure 4–3). While lines in various directions can be difficult to follow, this simplified notation can be more easily understood by those unfamiliar with looping activity behavior. In common parlance, a repeat means to do again and save the previous results; a redo means to do again and overwrite the previous results. Often, a looping subprocess is a better choice because it shows a repeating behavior instead of a redo.

The style shown in Figure 4–3 is typical of many BPM automation and workflow systems. Since the diagram represents a process model, not the people or systems performing the activities, this is often an appropriate way to model. A BPM/workflow system orchestrates activity. The BPMN diagram represents what the BPM system will do. Therefore, there is only one true participant: the BPM system. All other participants are out of the scope, and are not shown. For example, an HR role and an Accounting role do not interact in a BPM system. Instead, they interact through a system, that is—they use the system's user interfaces (UI's). Three pools can be used: the system, the HR role, and the Accounting role. Often, this level of modeling detail can be distracting or too nuanced. Both modeling styles will be discussed in Chapters 9 and 10. The modeling team should decide the needed detail levels.

The swimlane style of process modeling, shown in Figure 4–3, imitates workflow modeling styles of the mid 1990's. It is based on UML and traditional flowcharts, and is commonly used in human workflow diagrams. With roots in UML modeling, BPMN provides more detail. Often in BPMN, multiple pools are used to show the points of interaction and details of messages between participants.

A more modern style of BPMN process modeling can include a coordinator participant. The coordinator participant is a valuable abstraction. It can represent a computer system, a person, or an entire organization. The coordinator functions as the participant who is aware of all activity. They coordinate events across all other participants. Usually, a coordinator does not perform any of the tasks.

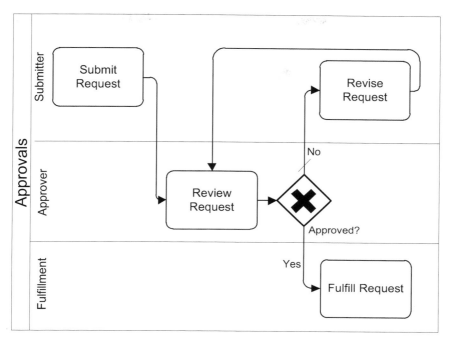

Figure 4–3   *Looping using upstream sequence flow.*

Instead, the coordinator dispatches tasks to other participants to complete. Figure 4–4 demonstrates a looping subprocess with a coordinator participant pool.

Process actors are shown using swimlane style modeling (as in Figure 4–3). Figure 4–4 shows the participants involved in the process—it also details how the participants interact. Figure 4–3 does not show the means of communication. For some process models, the interaction details might be important for synchronization purposes. For example, it might be important to show that a document approver is a person who is not normally involved in the full process. The approver must be alerted to do something. An alert implies an event, and a message interaction is the appropriate method of triggering an alerted action.

Figure 4–4 provides a more objective, focused process model, one that is simpler to create. When the coordinator is drawn first, as in Figure 4–4, design is faster and more complete. Additional participants (swimlanes) are filled in only after the process objectives have been properly diagrammed; one should focus on process objectives first. This is because an analyst who draws a swimlane (pool or lane) might assign activities to a participant. In contrast, an analyst who models the objectives first will carefully consider the inclusion of each participant, as necessary to support the process goals and objectives.

In modern process modeling, a coordinator participant will often represent an ERP, CRM, or other application that keeps track of process activity. Sometimes

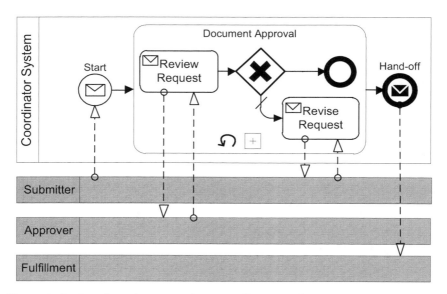

Figure 4–4   *Looping subprocess using a coordinator pool.*

this might be a BPM System (BPMS). The difference is that a BPMS has a more process-centric way of monitoring process activity and events. Naturally, it will have a higher participation level in the process. Applications, such as the ERP or CRM, tend to have a more passive role in a process design. They generally respond to user input. BPM systems produce and respond to events.

The message activities in Figure 4–4 are used for clarity and understanding. Note the two-way message flow. This is known as synchronous message flow. It designates a proper reply for the process to continue. Otherwise, the activity is not considered complete, and the process will wait. This pattern is typical when using the coordinator/dispatcher modeling style as in Figure 4–4.

Often there are many participants involved when the process design calls for looping or multiple-instance subprocesses. More participants require more pools and many participants cannot reside inside an expanded subprocess. Here, the modeling style in Figure 4–4 is required.

When used with different pools, the multiple-instance subprocess has some unique, implicit capabilities. The pattern shown in Figure 4–5 shows a voting process. First, a request is made for a vote from committee members. For each committee member, a vote request will be sent, and the process cannot continue until all members have voted.

The messaging pattern shown in Figure 4–5 is often called asynchronous, meaning that a request will be sent, and separately a reply will be made on another event. In contrast, Figure 4–4 shows a synchronous pattern which requires the process to wait for a reply before doing anything else. With asynchronous communication, the participant can do other activities between "request vote" and "receive vote".

The parallel multiple-instance subprocess pattern in Figure 4–5 is particularly useful and common. Depicting this process behavior with a looping subprocess adds more complexity. First, you must send a number of requests, and then later another subprocess that receives the same number of replies. Figure 4–6 shows a looping subprocess pattern solution.

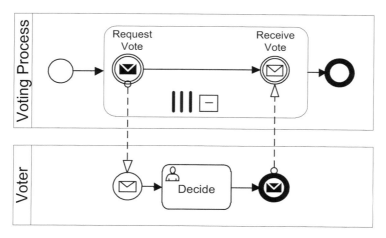

Figure 4–5   *Multiple-instance subprocess interaction.*

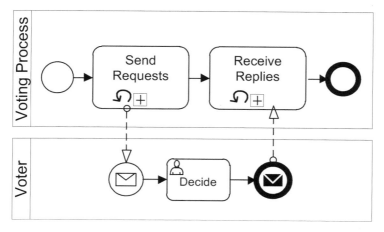

Figure 4–6   *Voting process with looping subprocesses.*

Since the looping subprocess is sequential, it can only interact with a single voter. By detaching the sending subprocess from the receive subprocess, Figure 4–6 mimics a parallel solution. This adds complexity for the reviewer and for the implementer.

The pattern in Figure 4–5 is simpler and better coordinates the voter response. In Figure 4–6, if a voter replies before all requests are sent, the reply is probably lost. Since each instance of the subprocess is running independently, in parallel, the parallel multiple-instance in Figure 4–5 fixes this problem. Here, the send and receive can easily be managed within a single scope, and clearly correlated.

LINK EVENT

There are two types of link events—intermediate catching and throwing,[1] as shown here.

The link event allows a diagram to continue onto another page. The link denotes a break in a sequence flow therefore there is no start event or end event. If a diagram page is to start with a link event, then use the catching (unfilled) intermediate link event. Use a throwing intermediate link event when the diagram continues on the next page.

Processes cannot start with a link from another page because the process is in a state of execution. The link shape marks a continuation point of a process. Similarly, do not end a process by linking to another point in the process. Once the process completes, it cannot resume. Therefore, only the intermediate link shapes make sense.

Figure 4–7 shows the proper usage of the link events. The process can be started by any start event. Alternately, the process can begin with the intermediate link event (catching). The gateway makes a decision to either continue in this diagram or continue on another diagram with the intermediate link event (throwing).

---

1. In the BPMN 1.0 specification, there was also a link start and link end event. The BPMN 1.1 specification removed the link start and link end event.

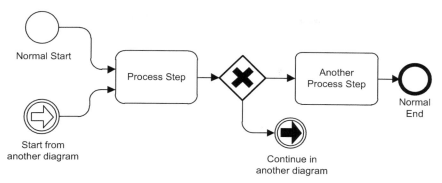

Figure 4–7 *Link event usage.*

The link event can be used to create jumps to another point in a diagram. This is often used instead of drawing lines because it creates a much cleaner diagram.

Figure 4–8 shows a hiring process which finds ten candidates and does initial telephone screenings. If the candidates have the necessary skills, they go to the interview subprocess. Sometimes, after speaking with the first ten candidates, not enough are found to start interviewing. If this is the case, the gateway "enough to interview" routes to "no", leading to the link event. The link points back to point A.

The candidate search is conducted in parallel with multiple recruiters (note the parallel marker on the multi-instance subprocess). However, the actual interview process occurs in series, one task after the other. The number of candidates is predetermined before the subprocess starts, so the multiple instance serial subprocess is used. After the first round of interviews, there could be one of three different outcomes:

1. All candidates might have been eliminated. In Figure 4–8, this would cause the second gateway to route to the link event, pointing back to point A.

2. There might be a need to interview candidates more than once to help with the decision process. The second gateway in Figure 4–8 would route to the link event that routes to point B.

3. (Default) Someone was hired. The process is complete.

MULTIPLE EVENT

There are many types of events in the BPMN 2.0 specification. Sometimes the exact event types are not known at the time of diagram creation. Other times, the event might be complex and it might not be a straightforward model with a timer or a message. For these reasons, there is an event with a multiple type (see Figure 4–9).

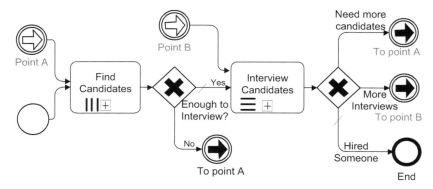

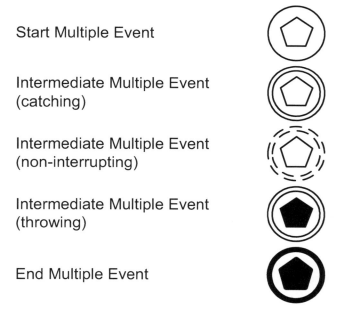

Figure 4–8 *Using link events instead of lines.*

Start Multiple Event

Intermediate Multiple Event (catching)

Intermediate Multiple Event (non-interrupting)

Intermediate Multiple Event (throwing)

End Multiple Event

Figure 4–9 *Multiple event types.*

Since they are abstract, multiple events can be hard to understand. Generally, a multiple event is "shorthand" notation for multiple events triggering a process. Triggers could include messages, timers, conditions, signals, escalations, and other event types (escalations and signals are covered later).

First, we must introduce the general purpose of the multiple event. Then, we will examine some of the complex use cases. Figure 4–10 shows an example of using generic events instead of specific types.

Figure 4–10   *Drawing generic events with the multiple shape.*

Importantly, any of the possible events within a multiple event could trigger the start event. Since one event triggers the transition, this is also known as exclusive behavior.

There is another multiple event type with inclusive behavior (all events required) that will be discussed later.

Potentially, the end event in Figure 4–10 could throw any event, but it only throws one event instance (not many events simultaneously). With this shape, the type of event is undefined—it could be a message, timer, or any other thrown event. Later we will discuss this more in detail. This concept is relevant to understanding the event-based gateways.

EVENT-BASED EXCLUSIVE GATEWAY

In Chapter 2, we introduced the data-based gateways. Data-based gateway means that it evaluates a data condition, which then leads to a specific sequence flow path. For example, "hire the candidate?" could have answers such as "yes", "no", and "maybe". With event-based gateways, the decision is not related to data, but rather, to an event. For example, "offer letter response received" is a possibility. There could also potentially be a rejection letter or no response at all. Figure 4–11 shows an example of handling all three of these events from one gateway.

EVENT-DRIVEN EXCLUSIVE GATEWAY

If the process starts upon receipt of multiple starting messages with different data types, then use the event-driven gateway with intermediate message events.

As shown in Figures 4–12 and 4–13, the event-driven exclusive gateway is a diamond shape with either an inner start (single line) or an inner intermediate event shape (double thin line).

As the name implies, the event-driven gateway shape is a composite of both behaviors. The circle indicates that this gateway type deals with events. Inside the circle, there is a pentagon.The pentagon in BPMN signifies multiple types of events. The outer shape is a diamond, indicating the shape is a gateway, which deals with multiple potential sequence flow paths.

The event-driven exclusive gateway awaits the initial message or event. There is a typical pattern for this gateway. Events include regular messages, signals, and

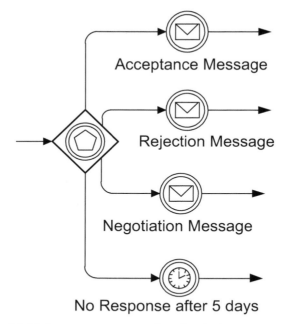

Figure 4–11   *Multiple events on an event-based exclusive gateway.*

Figure 4–12   *Event-driven gateway symbol (start).*

Figure 4–13   *Event-driven gateway symbol (intermediate).*

timers. Usually, messages and events occur before process gateways, so the notation may seem backwards; however, event shapes are drawn on the right side of the event-driven gateway or downstream. Placing the events on the left (upstream) side would be a series of events converging at the gateway.

The event-driven exclusive gateway can come in the start of a process, or in a sequence, as an intermediate shape. When the gateway is at the start of the process, the event shape inside the diamond is the start multiple-event (single thin line). Figure 4–14 shows the use of the event-driven gateway at the start of a process.

The gateway shape is a substitute for a start event. It awaits the activation of the downstream event shapes. In most process scenarios there is one defined start point, but with this gateway a process can start multiple ways.

When used as the start event, the event-based exclusive gateway indicates a new process instance for each event. In Figure 4–14, the receipt of a fax will create one process instance. A subsequent receipt of an email on the gateway would start a different process instance, separate from the instance started by the fax message.

In Figure 4–14, three different event shapes start the activities. For example, consider the email message event. There is a corresponding Receive Email step. Once an intermediate message is received and the process instance starts, it merges back into a people or systems process. Through one of many possible message types, the process initializes. Each message type requires different processing activities. Alternately, you can draw the process with a single message start, followed by a gateway that determines the message type received. The event gateway is a brief, explicit way of drawing this pattern.

Let's examine another use case that demonstrates the power of the event-driven gateway. The first activity in Figure 4–15, Call External System, awaits an answer from an external system. A message gateway awaits the system's response. The external system may be owned by another organization and controlled by their resources. This is a frequent scenario in today's networked business world.

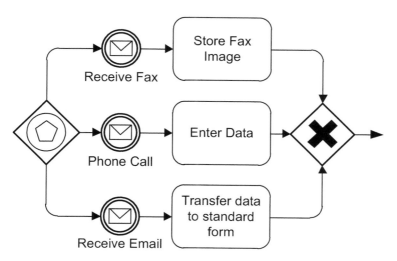

Figure 4–14   *Event-driven exclusive gateway used as a start event.*

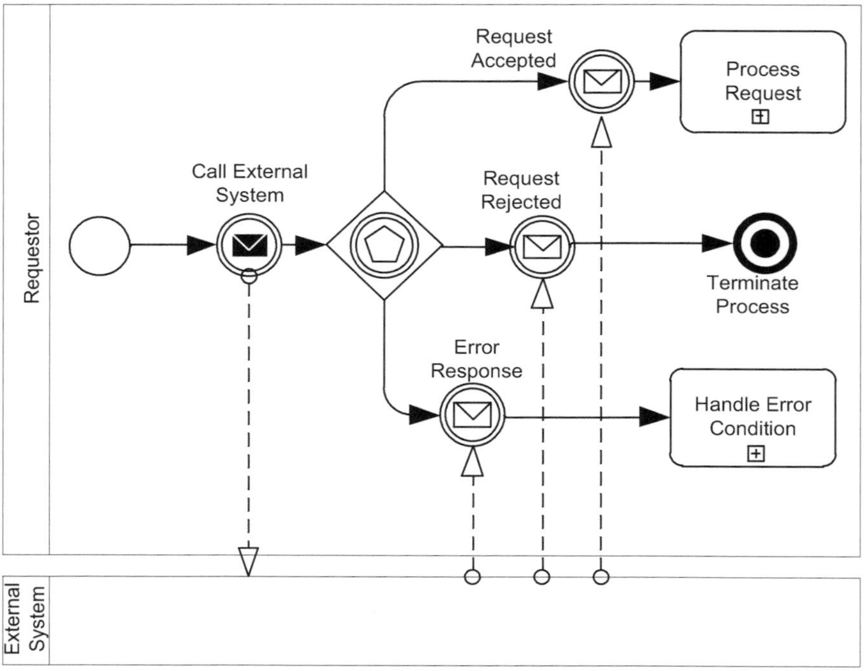

Figure 4–15   *Event-driven gateway used as an intermediate event.*

There are rationales for separating system responses—for example, a delay period occurs between sending and receiving the request. This is also an asynchronous interaction.

Another rationale is that processes might need to examine individual data types. In Figure 4–15, the external system responds with one of three different messages. Since the message format is different for each condition, three different message types receive the message. This pattern uses a single message event followed by an exclusive gateway. In many scenarios, different message types arrive from other participants and require mappings to the needed message types. If process message types are not exactly the same, use different message shapes combined with an event-driven gateway.

This process pattern is useful when there are multiple suppliers or partner organizations (external participants). Often, the external participant has varying degrees of system automation capabilities. Some external participants might support a Web services interaction, while others might support file uploads. Still others need support for a manual, or non-digitized, process. Each method of receiving input needs different incoming message processing. Therefore, the event-based exclusive gateway is an excellent choice for diagramming this pattern.

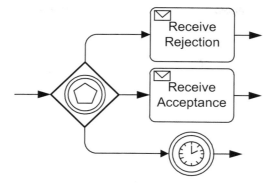

Figure 4–16   *Event-based gateway with message task and timer event.*

The event-based gateway can use a message task in place of a message event. This notation can be used in conjunction with other events, such as a timer or other message events.

Figure 4–16 shows an example of message tasks used with a timer event. The process will either receive a rejection letter or an acceptance letter, or, after the specified time has passed, the process will continue without either message.

EVENT-BASED PARALLEL GATEWAY

In some cases, a process will need to receive multiple events before proceeding. By multiple events, a completed set of events must be completed, in some way. This is the purpose of the parallel version of the event-driven gateway (event-driven parallel gateway). Its shape is a white (unfilled) plus sign inside either a single (start) or double (intermediate) circle, inside a diamond (see Figures 4–17 and 4–18).

The pattern for the parallel event-driven gateway includes a parallel gateway for the merge. Alone, the event-driven gateway is never used for a merge; therefore a standard parallel gateway is used instead. It is a best practice to always include the merge immediately following the connected events. This will help eliminate confusion for those who are not familiar with this pattern.

Figure 4–19 shows that more than one message is to be received, plus another condition satisfied. If any of the events are not yet triggered, the process will not proceed. For example, the pattern could include an approval process with mandatory responses from two reviewers, and a business day constraint on the activity. When the second message was received on a weekend, the business day condition would not be true until Monday morning. Then, it would trigger the condition, causing the process to continue.

When used in an intermediate context, there is little difference between an event-driven parallel and a standard parallel gateway; however, when used in a process start context, there is a subtle but fundamental difference. An event-based

Figure 4–17   *Event-based inclusive gateway (parallel) start.*

Figure 4–18   *Event-based inclusive gateway (parallel) intermediate.*

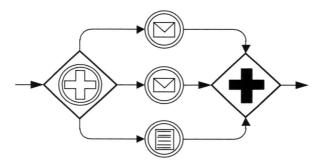

Figure 4–19   *Usage pattern for the event-based inclusive gateway.*

gateway for this pattern documents a process that does not start until the events are received. However, the ordinary parallel gateway signifies that the process has already begun, and must now wait for the events. An instance of the process would not emerge until all the events occur. With a parallel gateway, the process instance will be running.

The intermediate version of the parallel event-based gateway can be used for documentation, and to limit the scope of the subsequent flow to include events. Importantly, processes change over time and BPMN includes several ways of expressing the exact process behavior.

Figure 4–20 shows a pattern that starts a service order process. This particular process starts is a unique way. Both a purchase order and a signed statement of work are required before the process can start (messages received). In addition, the account must be in good standing (a condition). If all three of these conditions are not met, the process will not start.

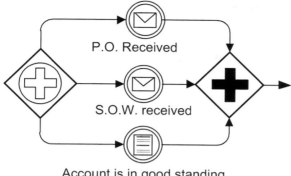

P.O. Received

S.O.W. received

Account is in good standing

Figure 4–20   *Parallel event-driven gateway as a start event.*

Without the event-driven parallel gateway, the example in Figure 4–20 would be more complicated to depict in BPMN. It is not known before the process starts which message will be received first. It is also not known whether or not the account is in good standing, which might change before or after either of the messages is received.

SUMMARY

We covered some of the more powerful shapes in BPMN. These shapes are composites of the behaviors and notations we have described in the previous chapter.

Looping activities provide important capabilities for processing sets of records or executing until a condition is met. The most common loop notation is shown here.

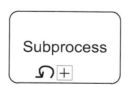

BPMN provides the link event to simplify large diagrams. There are two types of link events—intermediate catching and throwing. The shapes are shown here.

There are many types of events in the BPMN 2.0 specification. All of them are shown in Figure 4–9.

The event-based gateway solves a common, yet complex scenario. When a process should start upon the receipt of multiple starting messages with different data types, it should use the event-driven gateway with intermediate message events. The event-driven gateway shapes are shown here.

These shapes and their use are a bit advanced, yet they are composites of the fundamental set we have discussed. In order to model more complex business processes, you will need to know these. In the next chapter, we will complete the tools you need to manage events.

CHAPTER 5

HANDLING COMPLEXITY

ERROR HANDLING, TRANSACTIONS, MULTIPLE EXCEPTIONAL FLOWS, AND COMPLEX MERGES

Previously, we described the core building blocks that make up process flow in BPMN. When used with the shapes and patterns introduced in this chapter, BPMN can model increasing complexity.

Simplify Complex Merges with Subprocesses

A process model might have a number of gateway paths that include a composite of exclusive, inclusive, and parallel transitions. These can be merged with a BPMN concept known as the complex merge. The shape for complex merges is called a complex merge gateway. The complex merge gateway is a diamond shape with an enclosed asterisk, as shown here.

A complex merge situation usually occurs because of poor gateway pattern usage. Consider Figure 5–1 where a complex merge is used.

Since it can be confusing, use of this shape is not recommended; it might require the reader to backtrack. The same pattern created by the complex merge gateway is presented through different means in Figures 5–2 and 5–3. All the logic

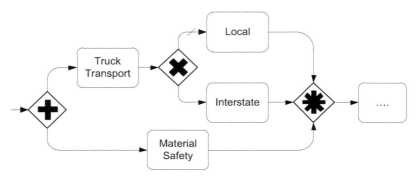

Figure 5–1   *Usage of the complex merge gateway.*

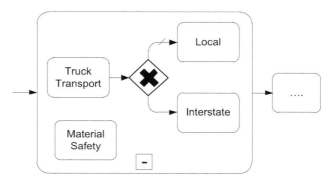

Figure 5–2   *A complex merge pattern using a subprocess.*

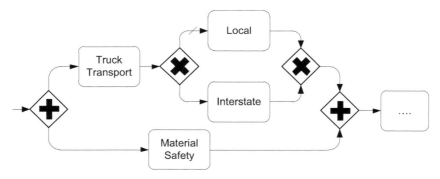

Figure 5–3   *A complex merge pattern solved with explicit merge points.*

from a complex merge shape can be defined in a subprocess (Figure 5–2). Without the subprocess, you can use explicit merges (Figure 5–3).

Since subprocesses have an implicit parallel split and merge, the subprocess can solve complex merge challenges. Even without the complex merge, a subprocess might be suggested for the scenario in Figure 5–3. We recommend avoiding using the complex split and merge, and, instead, using the subprocess to accomplish the diagram's objective. For instance, the patterns in Figures 5–2 and 5–3 are equivalent. Figure 5–2 is more compact and uses a subprocess implicit split and merge pattern.

To improve clarity in Figure 5–2, consider a parallel gateway before the "Truck Transport" and "Material Safety" activities, and leave the rest unchanged. Either way, the meaning is unchanged. With this thinking, it can be easy to find implicit split and merge patterns in the subprocesses. Outside a subprocess, use explicit splits and merges.

When choosing a pattern, pose the question "will adding the explicit splits (or merges) add clarity to my diagram or will it add clutter?"

Error and Escalation Events

The error event shapes either generate an error flag to be raised, or catch and handle an error condition. A throw is when an error condition is raised. That is, the error throws the condition. Then, the error condition is caught by another shape. The error event shapes include the intermediate error event and the error end event. As with the message intermediate events, there are two variations of the error intermediate event—the unfilled (white) icon for the catching version, and the filled (black) icon for the throwing version. The intermediate, throwing, catching, and ending error events are displayed as shown in Table 5–1.

An escalation is very similar to an error event. Escalations represent a condition created inside the process that must be handled outside the normal flow. An escalation event denotes that, while performing a task, this escalation can be issued to trigger the actions specified in the diagram. The task can be cancelled or other activity flow can take place in parallel. An escalation denotes a more ad-hoc or looser process flow.

Similar to the error intermediate events, there are three variations of the escalation intermediate event—the unfilled (white) icon for the catching version, and the filled (black) icon for the throwing version. There is also a non-interrupting variation. The shapes are shown in Table 5–2. Like the timer event, error and escalation events can be connected to a subprocess or to a transition (see Figure 5–4.)

Modeling Error Handling

The exceptional condition path might contain multiple steps that handle the error. We recommend grouping multiple steps in the exceptional flow into a subprocess, as in Figure 5–5.

Exceptional flow for errors is always interrupting; the subprocess that generated the error will terminate, and the alternate "exceptional flow" is followed instead. Later, the process can merge exceptional flow with the main flow. The exceptional

Table 5–1   Error Intermediate Events

Start Error Event (catching)	
Intermediate Error Event (catching)	
Intermediate Error Event (throwing[a])	
End Error Event	

a.   BPMN 1.0, 1.1, and 1.2–Removed in 2.0

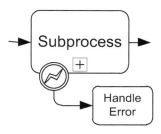

Figure 5–4   *Basic exception-handling flow.*

flow merge does not need to immediately return to the subprocess that generated the error. If required, a process model can merge several steps downstream. When merging, however, special precautions should be taken. Interrupting flow should always use exclusive merge patterns—either implicit, as shown in Figure 5–3, or with the addition of an exclusive gateway at the merge point, as shown in Figure 5–6.

Since exception handling always interrupts every activity in the subprocess, the subprocess generating the error is always cancelled. Another challenge is that

Table 5–2   Variations of the Escalation Intermediate Event

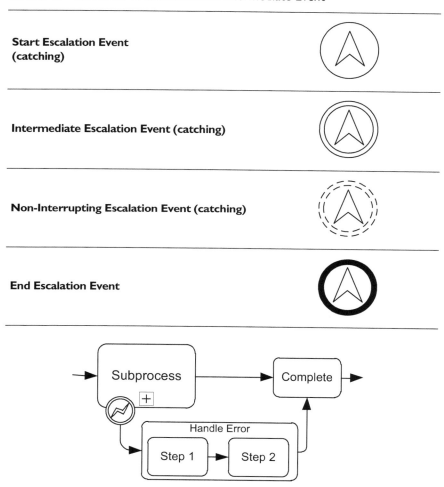

Start Escalation Event (catching)	
Intermediate Escalation Event (catching)	
Non-Interrupting Escalation Event (catching)	
End Escalation Event	

Figure 5–5   *Using subprocess for exceptional flow.*

the data-handler scope does not have access to its parent scope. That is, the values of the data in the subprocess are not available to the catch handler. Therefore, any data generated in the subprocess might be lost if the error occurs before a save. To retain data in the event of an error, there must be a start error event.

Figure 5–7 shows an event subprocess. An event subprocess is illustrated with a surrounding dotted line border. This subprocess type can only be used for catching events. An event subprocess always starts with a catching start error event. In contrast, events on a subprocess border serve the same purpose but always catch with an intermediate event.

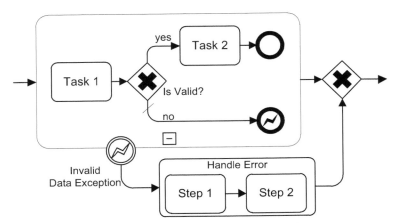

Figure 5–6   *Subprocess scopes and error handling with explicit merge.*

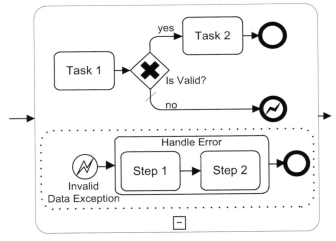

Figure 5–7   *Exception flow inside the subprocess with start error event.*

As shown in Figure 5–7, the start error event can only be used in a subprocess that has the potential to throw an error. A process should not start a flow in a pool with a start error event, and you cannot start normal flow within a subprocess. The start error is only used for exceptional flow within a subprocess.

The exceptional flow shown in Figure 5–7 cannot merge with any other flow inside the subprocess. The subprocess acts as an implicit merge point, because all activity inside a subprocess must complete before subsequent activity will activate.

Exceptional flow inside a subprocess has access to the same data and conditions as its parent scope. Therefore, in Figure 5–7, any data created while executing tasks 1 or 2 would be accessible to the error handler. In contrast, steps 1 and 2 of the error handler in Figure 5–6 require special handling of the data. This will become a more important concept later as we discuss transactions.

Process models often specify error conditions with a pair—a throwing end error and a catching intermediate error connected to a subprocess. End error events, not handled in the scope of the subprocess or larger process, do not need this matching intermediate process.

Errors arise from a number of conditions. Web services and databases might be offline for longer periods than specified by a "service-level" requirement. Data from employees or trading partners might be incorrect. Errors can be detected in the process data through business rules or in combination with different events in the process. It is often necessary to define a number of errors for different conditions.

Error events throw variables that can be caught by subsequent intermediate errors. In a subprocess, different error handling procedures are needed for different conditions. Figure 5–8 shows a process with multiple error handlers for different conditions. One condition merges with the main sequence flow. The other error event handler causes a link event, which implies a loop back to the start of the subprocess.

Escalation: Contrasting Merge Patterns

When there are non-interrupting events involved, merging exceptional flow with normal flow can be especially challenging. Figure 5–9 shows an example of an explicit merge on an exclusive gateway after an interrupting event. It is not possible for more than one interrupting event to be triggered, because the parent scope would be cancelled. Therefore the exclusive merge is the best design approach.

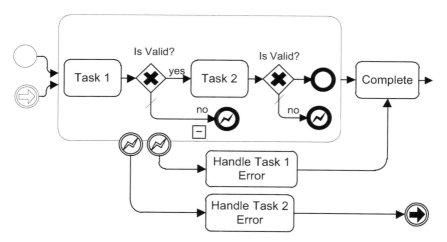

Figure 5–8   *Multiple error handlers on a subprocess border.*

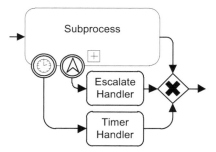

Figure 5–9   *Interrupting merge pattern.*

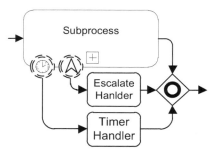

Figure 5–10   *Non-interrupting merge pattern.*

When non-interrupting events are introduced into the pattern, pay close attention to how the paths merge. The non-interrupting exceptional flow need not merge with normal flow; it can simply end. Yet these paths merge in parallel. Figure 5–10 shows this pattern. Since all paths are active, parallel gateway would not handle the exception. The exclusive gateway would not work because more than one path could potentially be active. Therefore, the inclusive gateway is the best choice.

More complexity arises when error handling combines interrupting and non-interrupting events on the same subprocess. Figure 5–11 shows this hybrid merge pattern.

Figure 5–11 solves the problem of combining interrupting and non-interrupting events. But what if the interrupting escalation occurs after the non-interrupting timer? Should the timer handler continue? In Figure 5–11, the timer handler would continue until completed, regardless of the state of the escalation handler. This may or may not be the desired behavior.

Figure 5–12 shows the hybrid merge pattern using a subprocess for the non-interrupting merge condition. The timer event is non-interrupting. Therefore, it can occur in parallel with the normal activity. The interrupting escalation condition is handled with a standard exclusive merge pattern, external from the subprocess. In this case, if the escalation event is thrown from the activity, enclosed in the subprocess, the entire parent subprocess cancels along with the potential

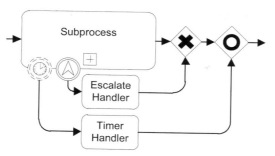

Figure 5–11   *Hybrid merge pattern.*

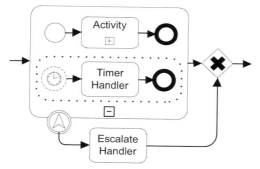

Figure 5–12   *Using a subprocess to solve merge challenges.*

timer event. Therefore, the timer, its corresponding event subprocess handler, and all activities are cancelled when escalation occurs. The escalation event has full override capacity, including any enclosed non-interrupting events and exceptional flows contained within the subprocess.

In perhaps the most difficult pattern to understand, the subprocess in Figure 5–13 is a hybrid of interrupting and non-interrupting events merging. Start events are used for both exceptional condition handlers. The subtle difference between the normal start, non-interrupting, and interrupting events might be easy to miss. Therefore we only recommend using this style with advanced teams.

The pattern in Figure 5–13 is nearly identical to that of Figure 5–12, with one small difference. Both event handlers are using an event subprocess, contained within the parent subprocess. The escalation handler activity has access to the same data scope as the other activities contained in the top-level subprocess.

The modeling style in Figure 5–13 is most useful when an immediate merge is desired, as this style is simpler to draw than the style of Figure 5–12. However, processes cannot merge upstream in this process, as shown in Figure 5–14. So, sometimes the best design choice for these event handlers depends on the design intents, after the event is handled.

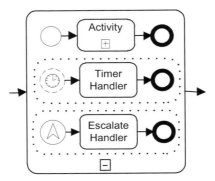

Figure 5–13   *Using start events as exceptional condition handlers.*

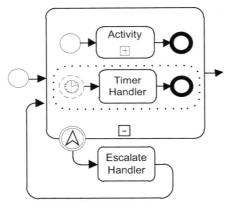

Figure 5–14   *Upstream flow with an event handler.*

The escalation event handler in Figure 5–14 is designed to route an activity to someone else, possibly a manager. After the manager determines the course of action, the subprocess will reset back to its previous state. For example, the manager decides, then routes the activity back to the work queue for all customer service agents. There should only be one instance of the enclosed activity occurring at once. To prevent the possibility of multiple instances in parallel, an interrupting border event handler is used. Now, the parent subprocess is cancelled, and a new one is created when the subprocess is restarted.

It is important to know what events can be used as non-interrupting. The following tables (Table 5–3 and 5–4) show what shapes can be used in each situation.

In subprocess interrupting, the shape can be used inside of a subprocess as an event handler. When used as event handlers, the sequence coming from the event is exceptional flow.

Table 5–3   Start Event Usage

Event Type	Start Events		
	Top Level	Subprocess Interrupting	Subprocess Non-Interrupting
Empty	√		
Message	√	√	√
Timer	√	√	√
Error		√	
Escalation		√	√
Cancel			
Compensation		√	
Condition	√	√	√
Signal	√	√	√
Multiple	√	√	√
Parallel Multiple	√	√	√

Table 5–4   Intermediate Event Usage

Event Type	Intermediate Events		
	Top Level Catching	Subprocess Boundary Interrupting	Top Level Throwing
Empty	√		
Message	√	√	√
Timer	√	√	
Error		√	
Escalation		√	√
Cancel		√	
Compensation		√	√
Condition	√	√	
Link	√		√
Signal	√	√	√
Multiple	√	√	
Parallel Multiple	√	√	

Not all start events have both interrupting and non-interrupting capability. For example, Error and Compensation events are always interrupting. Also note that some events shapes do not have a start event, such as Cancel, Link, and Terminate.

A subprocess boundary means that the shape can be attached to a subprocess border. Note that not all shapes have both interrupting and non-interrupting capability. For example, Error and Compensation events are always interrupting.

Top level throwing means that the intermediate shape can throw an event from within a sequence flow. Be careful when using this event type, because it might cancel the parent scope before subsequent downstream activity can occur. Intermediate throwing Signal, Link, and Message events are common in normal flow. Otherwise, you might want to use the event with non-interrupting exception flow.

BPMN Transaction Handling Mechanism

Transactions have a special notation that is different from event and activity BPMN. First, a transactional subprocess with a double-line border denotes the transaction. Inside a transaction activity, special activities called compensators are used to "roll back", or reverse, a previous action performed. The compensators can be triggered in two ways: either by explicitly throwing a compensation event, or by implicitly throwing a cancel event.

The double border also denotes that the process engine that runs the process will use a transactional algorithm to the events. Usually this has ACID[1] (atomicity, consistency, isolation, durability) properties that guarantee that database transactions are processed reliably. The syntax of the following BPMN shapes detail the steps of transactional assurance.

Compensation Events

There are four BPMN symbols for compensation events, as shown in Figure 5–15.

In addition to the events, there is a special activity type that is used for compensation handlers.

Some ACID activities create a specific output, or a committing of data that may need reversal if it is determined that a transaction should not proceed. The compensation event and compensation handling activities are used for this scenario. Compensation events are not used as part of process flow. Instead, compensation shapes use the association line. A compensation handler activity is an automatic activity that activates when a compensation event is thrown. A compensation handler activity can be a single task, or it can be a subprocess when multiple rollback steps are required for a transaction (see Figure 5–16).

---

1. ACID (atomicity, consistency, isolation, durability) is a set of properties that guarantee database transactions are processed reliably.

Figure 5–15   *BPMN symbols.*

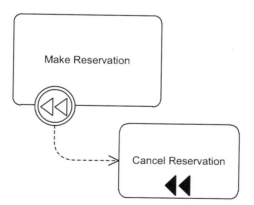

Figure 5–16   *Compensation intermediate event and an associated compensation handler task.*

Processes often produce groups of transactions, in databases or application services, called nested transactions. A set or nesting of these transactions is called a savepoint. In rollbacks, transactions at a savepoint are removed. The compensation event shapes include the intermediate compensation event and the compensation end event. A pair of shapes specifies a compensation condition: an end compensation and an intermediate compensation connected to a subprocess.

There is no compensation start event. Like the error event, a process cannot start with a compensation event. Optionally, the compensation end event shape can indicate a distributed transaction rollback. Use of the end compensation event is an explicit way of causing compensation. Compensation events can also be implicit within the scope of a transaction. If a transaction were to fail, all compensation handlers within a transaction subprocess should automatically start the rollback steps associated with each activity inside the transaction.

BPMN treats each subprocess as a separate, long-running transaction. The transaction records all sequences of activities. Since transactions in a business-process approach might require lengthy periods to complete, traditional mechanisms for saving database data are not always appropriate. As the process executes, data might be saved to one or more (even many) databases. The idea of the long-running transaction relies on grouping these databases into smaller transaction sets. Therefore, your process must undo the partial results of a failed subprocess.

Compensation handlers reverse the effect of a finished unit of work in a business process. However, because a process is not aware of the details of a database transaction, the model must specify how the reversal happens. The process invokes the compensation when an error or unexpected condition arises during the normal work of the process. This cleans up the process for the compensation handler to start its reversal activity.

As an example, suppose I want to have a peanut butter and jelly sandwich. I can't make this sandwich unless I have peanut butter, jelly, and bread. I won't know that I don't have the three items required until I go to retrieve the items. If I don't have all the required items, then I must return the other items. Errors might occur in this scenario, such as the bread being stale. (See Figure 5–19)The model either associates each activity with an inverse action when the transaction fails, or uses a subprocess to handle all compensation in one handler activity. Either way, the association dotted line is used instead of the sequence flow solid line. Individual compensation handlers are used in this particular case because each activity requires a specialized inverse activity to compensate for the transaction failure.

Cancel Events

There are two cancel events, the intermediate and end cancel event, as shown here.

The cancel events are used with a subprocess that processes a transaction. There are only two types—the cancel end event that throws the condition and the cancel intermediate event that catches the condition. The cancel intermediate event can only be placed on the border of a subprocess.

The cancel end event is used when a condition is discovered that does not require compensation, but will cause the transaction to cancel. In Figure 5–17, we show the proper usage of the cancel event shapes. When we try to update a database record that does not exist, we just cancel the transaction.

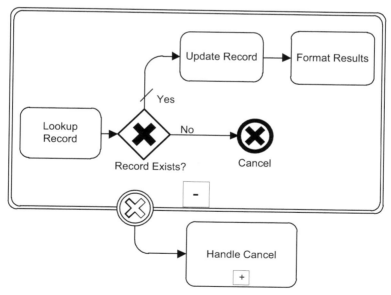

Figure 5–17 *The use of cancel events.*

Be sure to use the cancel event properly, and do not confuse it with compensation events. Compensations back out transactions with reverse steps where data is partly written.

The cancel end event is similar to the terminate event. The cancel event, however, does not terminate the entire process—just the surrounding subprocess. If the model's objective is to stop all activities in the entire participant pool, use the terminate event instead.

Figure 5–18 shows the combined use of cancel and compensation. An activity inside the transaction subprocess requires compensation when the transaction fails or cancels. The end cancel event throws, and the intermediate cancel event on the subprocess border catches.

The sequence flow from the intermediate cancel event leads to an exception flow that notifies the customer, then cancels the entire process with the terminate event. Since the compensation handler is inside a transaction subprocess, the compensation should automatically take place if the transaction is rolled back. A compensation end event could be used in place of the cancel end event, but this only allows one activity to be associated with compensation. All other intermediate catching events allow for sequence flow.

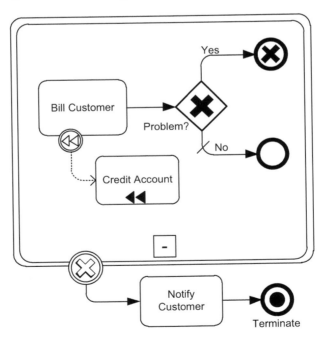

Figure 5–18   *Combined usage of cancel, compensation, and terminate events.*

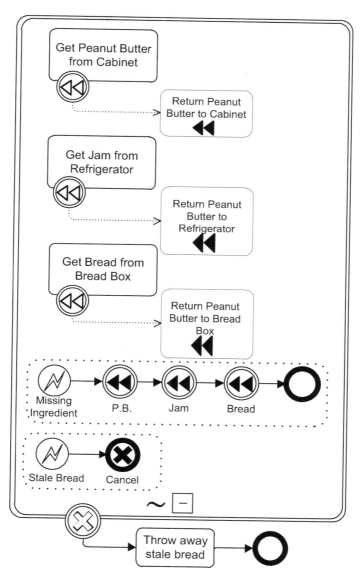

Figure 5–19   *Transaction subprocess containing compensation events and associated compensation handler activities.*

Figure 5–19 shows two ways of triggering compensation. The missing ingredients error starts an exceptional flow which triggers each compensation explicitly and separately. The stale bread exception flow throws a cancel event, which implicitly causes all compensators to trigger. The cancel event is also caught on the transaction subprocess border, leading to the final activity "throw away bread". When all of the compensators complete, the exceptional flow, resulting from the cancel event, should automatically be triggered (see Figure 5–20).

Challenge

Try to reproduce the diagram in Figure 5–19 using only flowchart shapes, taking into account all of the various exceptional conditions. Also keep in mind the various loop-backs, active monitoring states, and dynamically parallel sequence flow for the various escalations. It's possible to create this with only flowchart shapes, but it would take several pages to complete.

SUMMARY

We covered the basics of complex merges, error events, escalation events, compensation events, and cancel events. With the information in this chapter, you should be able to develop nearly production-ready processes.

With this last chapter in BPMN Shapes, we have completed our review of the BPMN 2.0 shapes. The key to understanding what these notations are is in the conventions of the markings. For example:

- Activities and subprocesses are rounded rectangles. Transaction subprocesses are double lined. Event subprocesses have dotted lines.

- Events are drawn as circles. The inner shape (message, escalate, timer, etc.) is the same regardless of the outer circle type.

- Events that are thrown are shown with black markers; catching events are white.

- Starting events are denoted with thin circles and ending events are denoted with thick circles. Intermediates are always double-lined.

- Non-interrupting events are dashed instead of solid.

Take care when leaving a subprocess via the boundary event. This chapter covered some considerations of how error events and non-interrupting events should be modeled.

This chapter's focus was on handling complexity, and as a process modeler, one must decide which style to use. We recommend using a high-level diagram with few details first, as in Chapters 2 and 3. Chapters 4 and 5 helped to define a more mature, production-ready process. The details are most often found in sub-

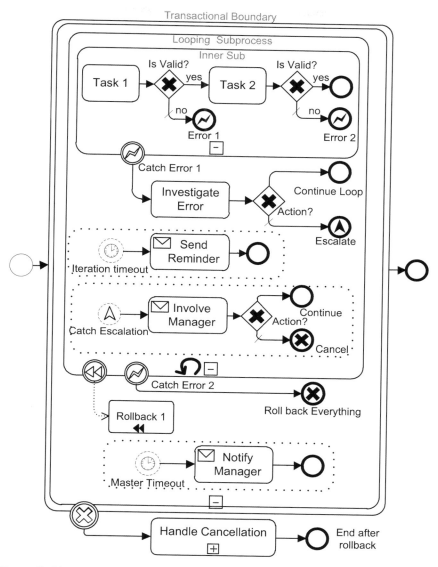

Figure 5–20 *The ultimate in complexity handling.*

processes, not at the top level. Refer to Chapter 9, PMF (Process Modeling Framework) to guide you through a structured process layout.

Some BPMN authors have used a token analogy for understanding the interaction of the process flow with the shapes. While some find this useful, we believe all that is needed is recognizing that a process naturally continues until it is complete.

As we mentioned in the introduction, process modeling in BPMN is a very powerful problem solving tool. Nonetheless, it is just one part of an integral view of the goals and objectives of the organization. There are other metaphors, namely business rules and events that will completely detail the activities of your process.

For the remainder of the book we are going to briefly explore process modeling in BPMN in the context of business rules and events. Finally, we will cover the Process Modeling Framework (PMF) and requirements.

CHAPTER 6

BPMN FOR DETAILED DOCUMENTATION

ARTIFACTS, DATA, AND CHOREOGRAPHY MODELING

Process modeling is a form of communication. To be an effective communicator, one must master the language. An effective communicator is often both descriptive and concise simultaneously. For BPMN process modeling, this means less words and more shapes. However, drawing out every detail in perfect BPMN syntax might not be effective either.

Up to this point, we have only shown the shapes associated with activity and event sequencing. BPMN includes many other features that are useful for documentation. In this chapter, we will introduce other shapes and modeling styles that might be helpful to illustrate more details about your processes.

Diagram Artifacts

There are three diagram artifacts—text annotation, data objects, and groups. Artifacts are often associated with other shapes, but they do not have a sequence or message flow. The dotted association line is used to attach text and data artifacts to other BPMN shapes. Association lines attached to a data object may have an open arrowhead which indicates data going into or coming out of an activity. (Be careful not to confuse the dotted association line with the dashed message line.)

Text annotations are particularly useful, as they can provide more detail about an activity than can normally fit into a label.

Text Annotation with more
details about an activity

Activities, events, and gateways will normally have a short label, as a good BPMN diagram should be concise. Another goal of creating a BPMN diagram, however, should be to minimize the risk of misinterpretation through better descriptions. Not all readers of a diagram will be BPMN experts. By using text annotations, a broader audience can be reached, while still using well-formed BPMN labels.

Groups

The group shape defines a common purpose to a group of shapes. The group shape is drawn as a rounded-corner rectangle with a dot-dash pattern, as shown here.

The group shape is permitted on the process diagram layer above pools and lanes. A group shape surrounds other shapes located anywhere in the diagram. A group illustrates related activities, even when they cross multiple participants (see Figure 6–1). As an alternative to a subprocess, the group shape might surround shapes inside the pool. The difference between a group and a subprocess is that a group does not have a process flow associated with it.

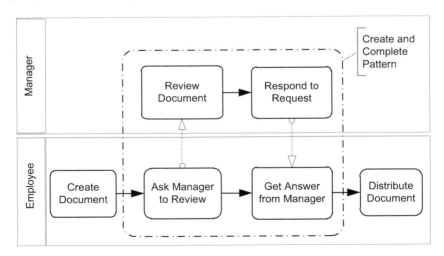

Figure 6–1   *The group shape encircles related activities in two participant pools.*

The data artifact is a rectangle with the upper right corner folded over, as shown here.

The text label for a data object can be found underneath the shape. Often, the current state of the data object is shown as an attribute shown in brackets under the text label. As the diagram progresses, the state of the data object can easily be read, as displayed in Figure 6–2.

As with the text annotation, the association line attaches the data artifact to another shape. Data artifact shapes are often associated with tasks, gateways, events, sequence lines, or message lines. In message flow, data objects portray the "payload", or content, of messages.

The use of data artifacts is optional. Some diagrams may concentrate on flow, while others show the complete details. Data artifacts provide more information without changing the basic behavior of the process, since they do not directly affect the sequence or message flows. A data object can be associated with an activity, which signifies where the data is produced. Associating data artifacts with a gateway can show the data on which a decision is based.

Data modeling is as critical as process, decision, and event modeling. A data object is a visual depiction of the modeled subject, or "business entity." A data model may depict an electronic form or a physical document. Data objects provide information about what activities need to be performed and/or what the activities produce. For instance, an inventory manager might requisition special items. The "requisition" would be a data item.

In some cases, the data artifact denotes more than one document. For this, BPMN 2.0 introduces the multiple data artifact shape. It uses the same base shape but adds the multiplicity symbol, which are three vertical bars. For example, a set of contract documents could be illustrated with the multiple data artifact symbol.

Contract Documents

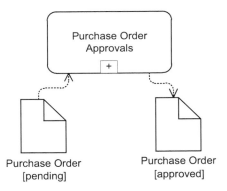

Figure 6–2   *Use of data artifact shapes.*

It might be beneficial to show the direction the documents are flowing. For example, are the contracts an input to the "Legal Approval" activity, or are they an output? This can be accomplished in several ways. First, the annotation association lines can have an arrow pointing to the direction of flow, as in Figure 6–2. But this subtle difference in line style might not be so obvious to the novice reader. Additionally, many modeling tools do not support this feature of BPMN.

The data artifact shape allows for additional annotation (an arrow) showing whether the data elements are being sent or received. Similar to the event shapes, the white (empty) arrow means receive and the black (filled) arrow means send. Figure 6–3 shows how these shapes are used, and how they can add clarity to a diagram.

The input and output annotations on the data artifacts can also be used in conjunction with the multiplicity symbol. Therefore, there are six types of data artifact shapes (see Figure 6–4).

Data Source Artifact

In some process models, an abstract data artifact might be inadequate to illustrate the details. The data artifact can represent documents, databases, or the content of message data. When there is a need to distinguish between these various artifacts, use these shapes, including the data source artifact and message artifact.

The data source artifact shown in Figure 6–5 is similar to a database symbol used in modeling notations other than BPMN. However, in BPMN the usage is more abstract. The data source is not always a database. Instead, it is a generic concept that represents a permanent place for data storage. This is because in the modern world of information technology, it is not always clear in what format data is actually stored, and often, it doesn't really matter. The actual means of data storage should be abstracted into a services layer, which is part of the Service Oriented Architecture (SOA) design. To a business analyst, the important detail is

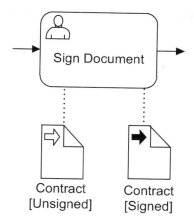

Figure 6–3 *Data artifacts as inputs and outputs to activity.*

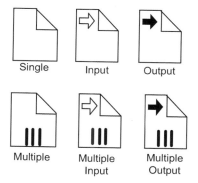

Figure 6–4 *Table of data artifact types.*

Figure 6–5 *Data source artifact.*

that the data is associated with permanent storage. The data is not transient. A simple data artifact shape does not have this definition.

A pool in BPMN implies that it contains data. However, when the data is persisted in a more permanent storage, it might be useful to show this detail. This clearly indicates that the data is available to other people and systems outside of the process context.

The data source artifacts in Figure 6–6 illustrate the proper use of this shape. The process shown typically interfaces a business process with an IT service of some kind. It might not be useful to show all of the inner technical workings of a back-end system, but it certainly is useful to show that data is being stored somewhere outside the process context. Another example might be "update CRM system". The CRM system has an associated data source that is available outside the process context. Therefore the data source artifact is a good choice for illustrating this detail.

Remember that a data source is not necessarily a database; it can be an entire application.

Message Artifact

In contrast to a data source, a message is always transient. BPMN provides message shapes for use as artifacts. The message artifact shape is the same that is used inside a message event. This is called a supporting shape. It does not suggest any executing code or participant work. However, without the enclosing circle of an event message shape, the message is an artifact, and can be used as a free-standing graphical element.

Message

Message artifacts can be associated with any activity, event, or messaging flow. They cannot be associated with gateways or sequence flow. The direction of message flow can be shown by associating the shape with a message flow line.

Figure 6–7 shows the usage of the message artifact shape. The association lines (dotted) are used to create the relationship between the message and where the message is used. When the manager in Figure 6–7 sends a "work request message", it is received as a process start event. The manual task is in the work queue of the worker. When the worker begins the task, it becomes active. After the task is completed, the send notification event occurs, which sends the "completion notification" message.

Notice how the addition of the message artifacts and text annotation add more clarity to the diagram. It is important to add these small details because not everyone is a BPMN expert. Annotations and artifacts serve as small hints to the intentions of the process model.

Note that message artifact shapes are always white. Black (filled) events symbolize throwing or sending. White events represent receiving. Because they denote the contents of a message, artifact messages are white. There is a gray filled message artifact called a non-initiating message, which is used in Choreography modeling. Be careful not to confuse the white, black, and gray message shapes.

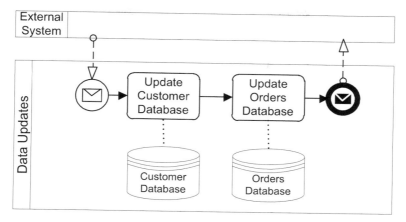

Figure 6–6   *Data source artifact used as documentation that the data is persisted externally.*

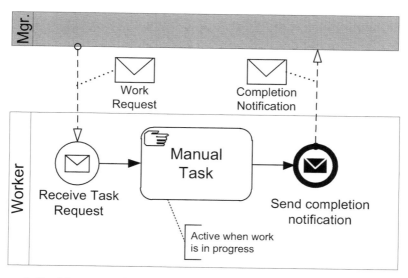

Figure 6–7   *Message artifact shape usage.*

PUTTING IT ALL TOGETHER

One purpose of using BPMN is to reduce text documentation that describes a complex process. To accomplish this, include as many details as necessary to illustrate the intent of the process, but not so much that the diagram becomes cluttered. The more shapes used, the less text needed. Figure 6–8 shows a process

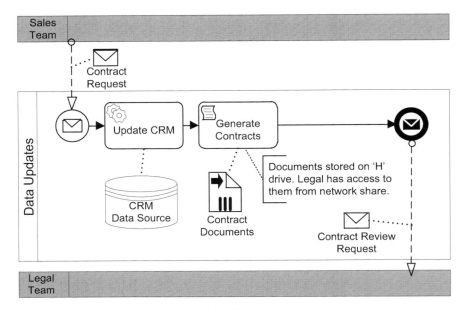

Figure 6–8   *Combination of multiple artifacts and annotations.*

where the sales team needs a contract reviewed by the legal team. The contract is not directly created by the sales team. Instead, the contract is generated by a system. First, the CRM data source is updated. Some additional information might be retrieved from the CRM system that automatically populates the contract documents. Contracts are generated, and the legal team is notified with a hyperlink that points to the document location on a network file share.

One could easily write out the details with a few short paragraphs, but frequently people only read text in the absence of graphical details. The graphical nature of BPMN is more efficient to read. In time, the eye is trained to pick out graphical symbols, and eventually the text becomes more difficult to read than the shapes.

Also, consider a multi-language environment If a person's native language skills are lacking, they can understand much of the process intention through the graphics without reading the text. Therefore, product manuals often include pictures and a few needed words. This same guideline applies to BPMN diagrams.

CHAPTER 7

BUSINESS RULES WITH DECISION GRAPHS

INTRODUCTION

As mentioned in the introduction to this book, the decision-centric, rules-driven process is an important usage pattern. Also, one frequent question that we hear is: "what is the difference between rules and process?" So, even though business rules are not currently a part of the BPMN spec, they are definitely a frequent part of process-modeling activities, and we feel it is very important to spend a bit of time on this topic. The business rules field is a broad topic with many approaches and objectives. In this chapter, we will focus on process-oriented business rules as they relate to process modeling.

Regardless of the process usage pattern, business rules are universally important, throughout every enterprise. Every moment, of every day, enterprise processes are used to make decisions that create value, expend resources, or affect risk exposures. Some of the rules that support these decisions are digitized, though many are manual. Either way, a standardized way of documenting these rules, from the perspective of process modeling, is needed.

Since they control an enterprise's most critical decisions, business rules have a huge impact on the overall efficiency and effectiveness of an organization. By supporting decisions, rules play an important part in the long-term governance of an organization's processes. For example, consider the rules for a manual decision within a process that is repeatedly performed in the same way. Based on process criteria (data, events, participants), these rules can easily support a digitized decision. Modeling and implementing the rules standardizes them—which is a strategic goal. By changing the rules, the digitized decision can readily adapt to current opportunities, market conditions, or other tactics. For any situation, improving the multitude of decisions that a process makes, by even a small amount, makes a huge impact on value, cost, and risk.

Most digitized decisions are implemented in computer code or spreadsheets. In some industries, it is a best practice to implement business rules in a business rules management system. However it is done, there are many advantages to separating the business rules from the process flow.

The methodology for capturing and digitizing business rules is known as the business rules approach (BRA). The approach has been adopted with varying degrees of success in many industries, particularly, health care, insurance and finance. Business rules can exist locally and be managed by the process owners. There are also global rules that should be managed at the enterprise level.

The business rules approach, using the visual method we will describe here, improves the visibility of processes' logic and computations. Centralizing the BPMN-focused management of your decision and business rules permits the discovery of rules associated with a particular decision or topic. This is an important characteristic of the visibility needed to manage high-performance organization.

Business rules and process-modeling capabilities are both adept at managing change. Process decisions are based on a set of logical conditions (rules). Sometimes this decision logic changes, but often the subsequent process flow does not. Likewise, sometimes the process flow changes but the decision rules remain unchanged. Change also has dynamic timing considerations. In some circumstances business rules change faster than the process. In others, the reverse is true.

For example, in the credit crisis of 2008, many financial institutions discovered that their risk models were hidden in a nest of impenetrable computed code or unmanageable spreadsheets. Financial institutions with visible, documented business processes and rules models were able to more quickly respond to the rapid changes in the economy.

Since the beginnings of BPM, the role of business rules has been acknowledged. For instance in their classic text, "Business Process Management: The Third Wave" Fingar and Smith state:[1]

> *Many corporations manage their business rules in a separate business rule management system ...*

The book initiated the idea that BPM, in concert with business rules, offered an agile approach to workflow and process integration. In a rules-driven process, wherever a decision appears, business rules evaluate the data provided by the process and control the basis for change in flows.

When we think of connecting a rule model with a business process, we often envision support for one decision. This is sometimes called a "process decision" or "decision activity". The common use for the outcome of a decision activity is to

---

1. "Business Process Management: The Third Wave", Howard Smith, Peter Fingar, Meghan Kiffer Press (October 2002)

control the outcome of a BPMN data-based gateway. Yet, as we will show, efficient, streamlined decision behavior often affects many parts of a business process.

In our process-modeling practice, organizations frequently present us with large spreadsheets and thick word documents containing a multitude of logic and computational steps. The logic within these artifacts controls or guides processes. It also frequently has process-control details. For example, the financial industry uses spreadsheets with a "score-card" model to decide a loan's risk. These models might include scores of computations, decision tables, and logic. As the risk of a loan increases, processes will start. For another example, consider the thousands of therapies, clinical procedures, and medical tests supported by medical insurance.

In this chapter, we will present a simple, visual way to model these rules-based decisions with decision graphs.

BUSINESS RULES AND
BUSINESS PROCESS MODELING

In a way, this chapter is about a single BPMN shape—the business rule.

The business rule task shape denotes the place within the process model which calls business rules and obtains the rules output.

The difference between process and rules is simple; processes are stateful and rules are stateless. Stateful means that over time, a process accumulates and retains data for each step. Stateless, however, means that after the logic of rule is complete, only the final outcome remains. The data used to arrive at the outcome might be recorded, but there is no time factor involved. A process has a start point and one or more pauses where participants interact. In business rules, there are no participants. A rule is an expression of a set or sequence of logical conditions. Similar to other process resources, rules are intended to complete nearly instantaneously, and then return a calculation or result to the process flow. The process flow then uses this calculation to affect process flow, participant assignment, or to manipulate process data artifacts.

The relationship between rules and process, from a graphical modeling perspective, is that a complex rule results in one BPMN shape. Often we see process models that show individual decisions as tasks in BPMN. This is incorrect. The proper way to model a decision-centric process is to use a single BPMN shape (rule, activity, or event). But this approach often does not provide enough detail. Therefore we introduce the graphical method for rules modeling.

Consider Figure 7–1. This simple process chooses which activity to run. The activity, Internal Transport or Contract Transport, will run for an indeterminate time. When the activity is done, the end is reached.

In our chapter on BPMN basics we discussed conditions. A condition is a true or false logical expression based on process data that controls a sequence of activities. A business rule is a series of conditions, often many, that evaluates conditions and assigns values to data. In Figure 7–1, a condition evaluated which path to take in the process. As demonstrated, business rules can be expressed verbally in English-like terms and stated with grammar. Alternately, you can visually express a business rule, by using the decision graph. Either way is adequate and many organizations have had success with written or graphical approaches. We will describe the graphical approach.

The decision graph is a visually connected set of conditions. To describe it we draw on some of ideas in BPMN—for instance the gateway, plus the general capabilities of the leading various business rules vendors, creates our visual notation. We present our first decision graph in Figure 7–2. The decision graph shows two conditions (diamonds) that assign values to data (square box).

A decision graph is a graphical representation. It is a map, or a type of graph of logic. Data from the process would provide conditions that point to either the internal conditions or the contract conditions. In a decision graph, the evaluation of the conditions is instantaneous.

Figure 7–1 and Figure 7–2 compare and contrast the similarities of BPMN and business rules. Both evaluate the logic conditions to decide which process activity or outcome to choose. The contrast is in the time element. This is what we mean when we say the process is stateful and the decision graph is stateless.

If Figure 7–2 denotes the rules for deciding the condition in the gateways of Figure 7–1, then you can use the business rules shape, as shown in Figure 7–3.

Figure 7–3 depicts the common view of the relationship between business decisions and business processes. Later, we will describe more usage patterns.

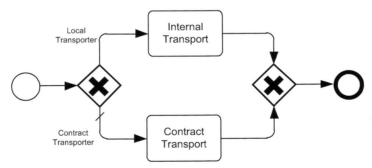

Figure 7–1   *Simple process with exclusive gateway, the process corresponds to the process: From the beginning, when a local transporter is used, do the internal transport task; otherwise when a contract transporter is used do the contract transport task.*

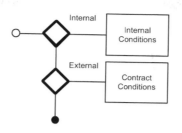

Figure 7–2   *Simple decision graph with two exclusive outcomes. The diagram corresponds to the logic: If internal then internal conditions else if external then contract conditions.*

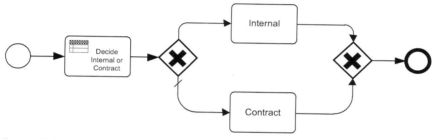

Figure 7–3   *An example of the business rule shape, shown as an intermediate activity.*

The distinction between stateless and stateful does not fully partition process and rules, and assigning the correct problem domain, requirements to process, or business decision logic is a question of design. There are times when a process makes stateless transitions in a sequence of gateways—at these times a process needs the same logic as a decision graph. For instance, process attributes might direct a transaction to accounts payable, or elevate an approval based on the size of the transaction—hence the overlap. Rule-supported decisions might need to "loop" through many records to compute a number, so there is an arguably short period of time between the start and end of the loop. Processes manage the concurrency of activities. The parallel gateway can "launch" activities in parallel (split) and wait or merge the activities when they are done.

In modern environments, where processes are automated, a highly decision-oriented process has copious process flow logic within the application. The logic includes both screen flow and the coordination of activity between multiple process participants. Most of the decision logic is managed separately in the business rules management system (BRMS). The decision shape from BPMN denotes this.

A business rules approach (BRA) effectively designs, organizes, and executes the logic behind a process decision. In addition to decisions, there are many other places where business rules perform logic. For various reasons, a process model might be started by or ended with a decision, as in the case of event processing. This will be covered in Chapter 8, Business Events and Business Event Modeling.

With an executable, decision-centric system pattern, decisions are often evaluated by a "rules engine". Chapter 1mentioned that processes contain data, but sometimes interact with other process data pools. Correspondingly, with this approach, a rules engine can interact with process data, or other external data. In the case of a decision-centric process, data is associated with a rule, but only temporarily, until the rule calculation is complete. Upon rule completion, the process absorbs the results of the rule as stateful process information.

For the purposes of this discussion, we will assume the rules engine has its own data pool. As mentioned in Chapter 1, the data elements in these pools are often referred to as business objects. Business objects are instances of types and can be as complex as needed to suit a model.

Even without seeking to create an executable or digitized process, the visual methods that we will describe are powerful tools for modeling, documenting, and visualizing business processes.

GRAPHIC NOTATION FOR DECISIONS

This notation is not yet part of the BPMN specification, but it is based on the efforts of the Production Rule Representation (PRR) community. The PRR community will be including this notation or a functional equivalent in forthcoming OMG standards. The notation is simple, vendor-neutral, and it is based on the conventions of BPMN (2.0). Within the framework of the logic of BPMN, we can explain some of the differences and similarities between modeling business processes and modeling decision and rules logic.

The decision graph will permit a limited analysis of our requirements.

Decisions

The foundation elements of a business rule, expressed in a decision graph shown in Figure 7–2, are the decision, outcome, and connector shapes. This is analogous to the foundational elements of BPMN, which are events, activities, gateways, transitions, and messages.

The decision is used whenever logic within a decision graph needs to make a distinction between two or more different situations. In general, with a decision graph, the decision shape runs down a sequence of distinctions. You use decision to evaluate multiple conditions; this is shown in the second shape. This is logically equivalent to the exclusive and inclusive data-based gateways in BPMN.

Unlike the gateway in BPMN, the decision-graph decision denotes the evaluation of a single condition. The shape is used to build up logic in a branch of exclusive logic in a decision graph.

The second shape is used in an inclusive branch, you might use this when multiple "if … then … else" statements should be grouped together. For example, suppose your spreadsheet was computing multiple values that control the process. Perhaps a condition would compute the price of an item in inventory, and a related, similar condition would decide the shipping time frame. You would use the inclusive branch to display this logic.

The objective of a business-rules model is to statelessly decide with data; while a process statefully coordinates the activities of participants (departments, users, and systems). So, a decision graph needs no equivalent for the parallel or complex gateway in BPMN.

In the previous example of large spreadsheets of logic and computations, one or more of the columns might become a decision. If the spreadsheet computes multiple rows then you use the inclusive. The condition that invokes the branch will reflect the logic and computations of the column.

Outcome

Logic is often referred to as statements of predicates in the form of "If *guard* then *outcome* else another *outcome*". The decision shape denotes the evaluation of a *guard*. The decision graph is a graphical representation of a nested 'If…Then…Else' statement. The outcome of the decision decides among conditions in the decision graph. Since it is stateless, the branch of a decision can end abruptly, with a decision outcome in the form of an assignment of values to attributes of a business object; or it can proceed to more graphical logic. We denote the action as a simple rectangle.

A

This outcome is the logical result of a truth condition, the guard, in the logic of the gateway. The outcome should set one or more data values within the rule engine's data area. Actions can also precede gateways. There are several other outcomes needed and these will be denoted with rectangles and markings.

Connectors

To construct the decision graph we need three additional features: a first connector, a last connector, and intermediate connectors. These are shown in Figure 7–4.

The first connector is the line with the open circle start. The intermediate line connects decisions and outcomes. The end connector is the line with the closed circle ending, and it can also connect to more decisions and outcomes. The end shape is optional and represents the else state of the decision graph.

As suggested by the definition of the intermediate connector, conditions can evaluate to branches of conditions.

With these three shapes, we can start building a decision graph that reflects an early business-rules modeling effort. Suppose we are deciding what mode of transport to ship cargo. Our choices are Local, Ground, or Air. Perhaps the cargo can be shipped in a rail mode. In this case, we still need to move the cargo to and from the rail terminal; so we create an internal branch of logic for this condition. This logic shows the ability to ship in tandem in truck and/or rail modes.

The decision graph is popular because it is a graphically concise form that is easy to understand. Even with non-abstract guards, the simple example in Figure 7–5 would require six sentences of "if-then-else" and could be complicated to read and comprehend. Yet, as we will cover in the requirements chapter, it is easy to graphically model a very detailed example by parsing the words of the business rules. In practice, a decision set in a decision graph can span many dozens (or even hundreds) of decisions.

In the decision graph, a stateless condition is modeled, so there is no need to merge the outcomes as with activities in a process model. Because it needs so many merging sequences, the equivalent BPMN diagram would be unwieldy.

Loop

Business rules often need to repeat logic across a set or array of records. Our simple decision graph notation supports loops with the shape.

Typically there are three kinds of loops supported in business rules: Looping while a condition exists, looping for a number of times with a counter, and looping for records in a list. The condition for the loop is defined within the loop shape. A record number or index would be managed by the specified condition. An example usage of the loop is seen in Figure 7–6.

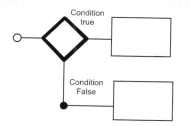

Figure 7–4 *Example showing decision graph connectors with an end connector and an "else" outcome.*

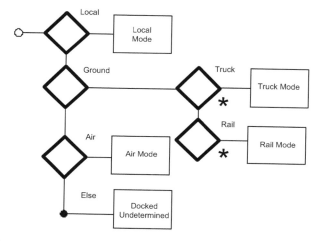

Figure 7–5 *A decision graph with a branch of logic that evaluates to another branch of logic.*

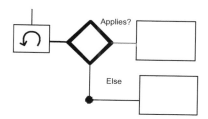

Figure 7–6 *An example of loop within a decision graph.*

The connector loops through a condition and if the logic of the decision applies then the outcome is applied. With the loop shape, our decision graph traverses arrays and vectors of records, and applies business rules. Such loops are important for developing complex algorithms.

For example, suppose your business rule is supposed to select the lowest unit prices from a selection of vendors offering the same material. You would use the several loops to find that minimum.

Map Outcome

Decisions graphs often need to connect the attributes of one business object to another business object. A map outcome denotes a mapping like this.

There are many industry standards for data exchange, such as XII XML standards, for data elements. Organizations that accept these documents must move and change this data to accommodate their business practices. For instance, if your decision graph must copy the value of attributes from an incoming order to a data element for posting into the ERP, then you denote this with a map. A map is denoted here.

Maps can be used anywhere that an outcome is used.

Rule Reuse: Reusable Subprocess Equivalent

The subprocess is an important shape in BPMN. We define an equivalent for our decision graph as follows.

Decision Tables

Decision tables are a very common business-rules metaphor. They are a compact way to show the same logic as a decision graph. They associate conditions with actions to perform. A decision table is useful when you have many symmetrical conditions that cause the same outcome.

Detailing the proper modeling and uses for decision tables is beyond the scope of this book; there are many other resources available for this topic.[1]

---

1. We recommend the research and writings of Prof. Dr. Jan Vanthienen:
   http://www.econ.kuleuven.ac.be/tew/academic/infosys/RESEARCH/PROLOGA/publications.htm

For the purposes of our graphical portrayal of a decision graph, we represent the call of a decision table.

Suppose we have a decision table that provides logic for moving the cargo with our internal resources. Then it would be useful to add this to our decision graph. In addition, there are conditions when special transportation for the cargo must be arranged. In Figure 7–5, the else of the central decisions calls another decision graph, and the local transportation calls a decision table; the decisions would appear as shown in Figure 7–7.

In business rules, the call to other decision graphs and decision tables enable the reuse of logic. This modular approach helps to create rule sets that are more easily managed. You can logically organize your logic with the decision graph, decision tables, and other flow rules. Sets of decisions can be federated, organized according to a topic or business area, or divided into areas of expertise.

EXCEPTIONS AND OTHERS

Even though they are stateless, decision graphs can raise and handle exceptions such as database errors, math errors, general business exceptions, etc. A decision graph should handle throwing and catching error events. Generally, BPMN

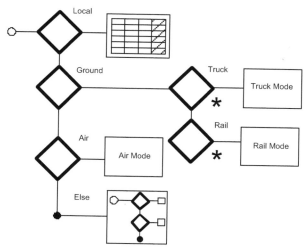

Figure 7–7 *A decision graph that calls another decision graph for special transportation and a decision table for local transportation.*

exceptions are connected to the boundaries of a subprocess. Similarly, in a decision graph, the exception might be connected to the end of the graph after the else-end shape. We have not described these.

There more shapes, not described, needed to completely denote a loop. These include immediate exit of the loop. It is not the intent of this Microguide to create a complete notation for decision graphs; however, our foundation of decisions, outcomes, and connectors is nearly complete. There a few more shapes needed and, for the sake of brevity, we will not present these. Among the shapes that we might add are:

- The service outcome calls an IT service such as a database query or a web service.
- The pattern-matching outcome will filter the business objects according to a query pattern.

With this simple notation, we have almost all of the tools we need to examine some use cases in the requirements chapter.

BUSINESS RULES USAGE PATTERNS

Business rules play an important role in the rules-driven process-usage pattern. As we mentioned earlier, the common conception of business rules is that they are only an element of a decision that affects the gateways of one process. However, researchers at Georgia State University and Utrecht University[1] have identified five categories of business rules that have a behavioral influence on the business process in terms of mitigating operational risk or achieving compliance to regulation.

The five usage categories are:

1. Rules for task sequencing
2. Rules for actor inclusion or task assignment
3. Rules for effect sequencing or gateway conditions
4. Rules for data or information registration
5. Rules for detection control or event responses

These five usage categories are briefly described here.

>   **1. Task Sequencing**—These rules influence the position of one or multiple activities, events, or decisions (and hence process elements)

---

1.   Zoet, Martijn, Richard Welke, et al. "Aligning Risk Management and Compliance Considerations with Business Process Development." Springer-Verlag, Berlin Heidelberg, 2009.

within a business process. Most often, to create a process that is compliant with the business rules, process elements are simply added, re-ordered, or removed. That is, the existing process model is updated to reflect the new rules.

2. Actor Inclusion/Interaction or Task Assignment—These are rules that influence the assignment of tasks or decision to specific actors. There are several approaches to creating a compliant process. First, defined actors, in the form of participants, can be removed, added, or appointed to different elements inside the process. In addition, processes can call business rules to delegate the activity to the correct actor.

3. Effect Sequencing or Gateway Conditions—These rules influence the paths chosen by gateways or conditional sequences inside the process. This is the classic pattern of the values, created by the rules, setting the conditions at gateways and directing the flow of the process. That is, the path chosen is directed by an evaluation of business rules associated with individual transaction. This is more dynamic than task sequencing, where rules influence the arrangement of the paths. An example of effect sequencing is a shipping process where, depending on the needs of the shipment, different transportation process activities need to be executed. This is the most common perception of processes and rules. To make the process compliant, business rules need to be enforced during runtime.

4. Data/Information Registration or Event Responses—These rules influence the recording and viewing of data and information, and the authorization to access it. Most often, to create a process that is compliant with the business rules, internal controls govern timing—for example, how long the recorded data must be kept accurate, and the predefined format of complete or registered data. That is, the registered data must contain the rules-specified information and authorization, restricting access to predefined user and roles.

5. Detection Control or Event Responses—These rules influence how a process responds to events. Events can be external or internal. External events might include weather or financial events. Internal events arise from the direct or audited results of an activity or processes. Most often, to create a process that is compliant with the business rules multiple solutions can be used. Process elements can be added, reordered, or removed. Also, we can have the process respond to an "event channel", or we can create a new business process to perform the event control.

Since a decision is made by many business rules, a decision can influence a process behavior in any combination of these ways. Moreover, as covered in the next chapter, event-based processing uses business rules.

Some of these usage patterns touch the process shape, while others act in different points in the application or process model. Understanding the relationship between the business rules' behavior and their influence on the process model and the enterprise architecture is important.

It is interesting to note that patterns 1, 2, and 5, do not involve business-rules methods. In these three, the business rules are implemented with changes to the process model.

There are three business rules patterns that connect business-rules decision graphs to business models: actor inclusion, event sequencing, and event detection control.

Actor Inclusion

The process might use business rules to decide what actor or participant can perform an activity. For instance, in Figure 7–8, a controller can call "actor rules" and decide which participant will be delegated the activity.

Figure 7–8 depicts the decision graphs as an associated decision graph. Depending on the actual technology implementation, messages might be used to pass data from the process to the rule and back. If this is known to be the case, you might want to use message lines to show this detail. Otherwise, we suggest using association lines. The association line implies a managed rule set that is associated with the rule activity but maintained outside of the process diagram.

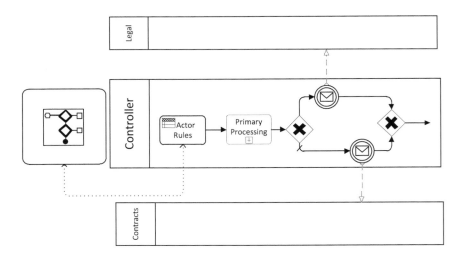

Figure 7–8   *For business rule pattern 1, actor inclusion, this controller process uses a decision graph to decide ('actor rules') which process participant is responsible for a part of the process.*

This notation is similar to how a document can be referenced in BPMN. The logic of the decision is documented by the decision graph and is stateless.

Effect Sequencing

Effect sequencing is the classic decision integration with a business process. The example from the first part of this chapter is shown in Figure 7–9.

Most business processes contain multiple decision integration points. Processes decide what discounts to offer customers, what benefits apply to an insurance customer, or which mode of transportation to use to ship a product. At these decision points, effect sequencing evaluates the data in the process. If you change the business rules in the decision graph, you will change the processes' behavior.

Event Detection Control

The event-driven process will be covered in the next chapter.

SUMMARY

A business decision is stateless and time-invariant. In decision graphs, business rules are adept at documenting and implementing complex decisions with clear, visual documentation. Moreover, business analysts can easily learn how to create and manage these decisions in business rules through visual metaphors, as they

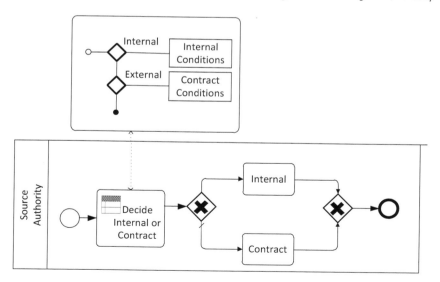

Figure 7–9   *For business rule pattern 3, effect sequencing, the sequence or path of the process is controlled by the decision graph.*

could in a process model in BPMN. Also, by providing a rules engine or other facility for decision graphs, the business analysis can manage complex logical decisions—those with a multitude of branches, loops, and decision tables.

Process logic is mostly concerned with coordinating and managing time-varying objectives and concomitant exceptions and states. BPMN is adept at managing organization and the interaction of activities. BPMN has time and error coordination elements. Many BPMN shapes, such as the timer, error and compensation events, have been designed to handle unforeseen process errors.

BPMN is designed to model and document an enterprises business process. To aid in modeling, most BPM tools can "play-back", or simulate, a process model for process verification.

Table 7–1 compares and contrasts the shapes on a decision graph and their logical analogies in BPMN. As discussed earlier, a decision graph is stateless and a BPMN process model is stateful. Both metaphors use logic conditions to choose an outcome or a path. The decision or gateway denotes a node of the condition's choice or path. Similarly, both metaphors need a start and a stop, a way to loop through records or conditions, and a call to other processes or rule sets.

It is difficult to manage dense, complex decision logic with BPMN. Decision graphs support organizational needs for business-rules modeling in a compact, simple way. BPMN supports the process automation abilities. Since the objectives are different, it is expedient to separate process logic from business decision logic.

Sometimes, the teams that maintain the business rules in an organization are different from the teams that manage the process. Often, in large corporate environments, there are many layers to the change management process. The objective of today's process and rules modeling is to end loose verbal or documented requirements gathering and cede control to the owners of the requirements. Therefore, one group of Subject Matter Experts (SME) uses BPMN to create processes, while another creates and manages the business rules.

Since our process-modeling approach is visual, logic for process and rules is expressed in the notations. Visual notation simplifies models and reduces the steps required to express, create, and update them.

In the requirements chapter we will provide more details about verbally parsing business rules. The approach we advocate in the coming chapters is designed to work directly with a set of simple graphical tools that empower managers and subject experts.

Process modelers and business decision modelers use the three metaphors of business processes, business rules, and business events to model solutions. As we've said before, business rules are easily modeled and understood with decision graphs.

In the next chapter we will cover the last of these three metaphors, the business event.

Table 7–1 Comparisons Between a Decision Graph and BPMN Shapes

Shape	Decision Graph	BPMN
Decision or Gateway	◇ ◇*	◈ ⊕
Connectors and Sequences	○— —| ●	○→ → →⬤
Loops	↺	↺
Rule Calls & Subprocess	(diagram)	+
No Analogy		
Decision Table	(table icon)	N/A
Maps	(map icon)	N/A
Outcome	A	N/A

CHAPTER 8

BUSINESS EVENTS AND BUSINESS EVENT MODELING

INTRODUCTION

As mentioned in Chapter 1, the business event is one of the three principal process modeling metaphors. Also, the event-centric process is a critical process usage pattern. Regardless of the process usage pattern, events, just like business rules, are universally relevant, throughout every enterprise. The events we focus on here are significant occurrences, mostly beyond the boundaries of the enterprise that affect its processes. These can be environmental, such as a weather shift, or economic, such as a change in commodity availabilities. More events might arise from political or social sources.

Event-based process modeling creates processes that are more aware. Hugh Brown, et al. state that "Events ... bring consciousness to the enterprise nervous system"[1]. Enterprise business events happen all the time. The challenge is to understand how some events are relevant to business processes and how they affect the outcome of processes.

By definition, companies with the best conscious awareness of events are the most competitive. Seemingly minor, secondary (micro) changes can have a quick and disruptive (macro) effect on business operations. Events signal changes that can profoundly affect products, services, customers, employees, and risk exposures. Only recently has the power of adapting to external change, through "event thinking", become a critical aspect of process modeling.

"Event thinking" is a shift from a focus on the internal processes to a focus on the external, non-process elements. Both viewpoints are reasonable and present

---

1. Brown, Hugh, et al. *Event-Driven Architecture: How SOA Enables the Real-Time Enterprise.* Addison-Wesley Professional, 2009.

different viewpoints of the same objective: the progress of enterprise activities over time.

- *The process viewpoint*—Depicts a preconceived map of activities with a set of pre-planned sequences. The process model is composed of activities, sequences, gateways, and all the other shapes.
- *The non-process viewpoint*—Focuses on distribution of states, random events, and activities.

In either view, the activities of the enterprise are identical. A process is an organization of things that should happen in a proscribed sequence. As a process becomes more organized, less unexpected events can be accommodated. With an event focus there are two distinctions:

- *Complex event detection*—It is possible for activities and responses to be expressed as a collection of organized events, but not necessarily as a process. We call this complex event detection.
- *Ad-hoc process*—It is also possible to have a disorganized process with no event sequence. We call this an ad-hoc process.

For business analysts, the event is a natural focus of a use case. Also, events accurately describe the phases of processes. Customer events include orders, receipts, payments, and returns. Similarly, supplier events include deliveries and invoices. With previous methodologies, these orders, receipts, and others would have been data elements, objects, and process activities. In BPMN, they can be activities triggered by the various event shapes. A process should be a natural flow of events: customer's orders lead to shipments, which lead to customer receipts.

The difference in process and non-process or even-based viewpoints can be seen in the basic process fragment in Figure 8–1.

The transition from the first activity to the second activity is presupposed or hardwired.

However, in Figure 8–2, we added intermediate message events that would emerge from a "cloud of events" and start the second activity. In the second activity, the activities of the organization would be the same, but the transition to the second activity would be initiated with a message flow that emerges from a consideration of external events. The difference with this approach is in the controlling logic that is monitoring events. Starting logic for the second activity could use internal and external events as input. Activities in the event-driven or non-process viewpoint are not predetermined—they are a part of a grid of potential event responses. Herein lays the dynamic nature of more dynamic processes.

In an event processing environment, modeling is different than modeling in a business process environment. We might use our BPMN shapes to model processes that anticipate conditions that might prevent the second activity from

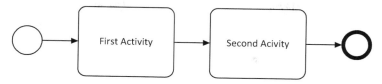

Figure 8–1 *A simple process fragment.*

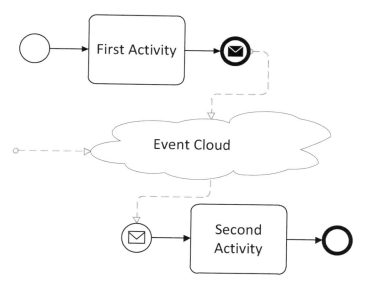

Figure 8–2 *Internal processes controlled by the external cloud of events*

taking place; however, the process design or the business rules must be changed to accommodate design changes.

Since events are not neatly organized, David Luckham[1] created the cloud analogy for the event space. According to Luckham, "[Events] do not necessarily arrive at the enterprise in the order they were created or in their causal order… they form an unorganized cloud of events".

Beyond sending a message to a process, Figure 8–2 raises a number of important issues. For example: How will the event capability decide what events to send to the processes? Can a process contribute events to the cloud? In this chapter we will touch on event processing as it relates to the process.

Ultimately, many advanced processes will consolidate all events into a single layer for maximum visibility and positioning for change. This centralizes control

---

1. Luckham, David. *The Power of Events: An Introduction to Complex Event Processing in Distributed Enterprise Systems.* Addison-Wesley Professional, 2002.

of critical events, and, because event monitoring is continuous and controlled by logic, rules-driven process control is also achieved.

This chapter introduces the effective and efficient methods needed to identify and address requirements arising from business events. First, to understand how business events are modeled, business rules must be understood. Then, events analysis constructs the requirements for business event processing. To support business responses and decision-making processes, event-driven processes leverage the information flowing through business systems and IT.

BUSINESS EVENT PROCESSING

Business event processing is a relatively new enterprise component. Nearly all components share the ability to recognize an event, identify that an actionable business situation has occurred, and coordinate the appropriate response (action). Event processing applies decision logic, in the form of rules, to one or several events, with the purpose of identifying the material events within the event cloud. Event processing detects, filters, correlates, and directs the appropriate messages to the correct channel. For instance, in an electric car owner's request for a charging point, an event processing point would seek an open slot (detect) and apply logic to the opening (assignment). In other scenarios, an event message could indicate that a commodity has reached critical price points, a trading partner is experiencing financial stress, or a security detector was activated.

Business Events Notation

Drawing on the previous chapters, a graphical depiction of basic event-processing concepts is shown in Figure 8–3.

Figure 8–3 shows an event detection entity and two reusable decision graphs from Chapter 7. The oval denotes continuous event monitoring and detection. Stateless logic filters and correlates the detected event. Events are then directed to the correct channel for receipt by a process.

In addition to business events, millions of potentially actionable events are flowing freely through the IT infrastructure. Since the proper response to these events is critical, event analysis is an essential part of process modeling.

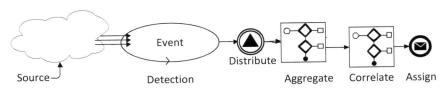

Figure 8–3   *Concepts of the atomic functions of event processing.*

Supporting the need for advanced event processing is a new and growing discipline. Organizations use the event-centric process pattern to interact and respond to a growing volume of business events and transactions in an agile, proactive way. Event analysis is an emerging area of business process modeling that develops support for the decision-based processing of enterprise-significant events. Since events can be produced by devices, it is also an increasingly vital part of strategies for the evolving "internet of things". The need for external event processing has increased as processes are discovered, mapped, and managed.

Business processes must accommodate event-driven, actionable situations. These include key events or combinations of events. The process model should be constructed to respond with the correct sequence of activities.

A thorough discussion of the Event Driven Architecture (EDA) is beyond the scope of this book; however, we will discuss the relationship between process modeling, BPMN, the EDA, and a number of business scenarios that implement event processing for improved decision making.

EVENT PROCESSING OVERVIEW

At an airport, flight delays and cancellations are common. But these events don't necessarily affect everyone; only those who are on the affected flights. This includes passengers, pilots, flight attendants, and ground crews. Other flights are also potentially affected by delays because an aircraft might still be at a gate when the next flight arrives.

Various means of communications are used to update passengers regarding flight status. The most obvious are the screens showing all flights and their statuses, which broadcast to everyone. There are also announcements broadcasted over the airport loudspeakers. In the security field, these displays and announcements are known as "mass-notifications". The monitors and the airport-wide announcements do not offer any guarantee that a specific passenger will receive the notification.

In an effort to improve processes and customer loyalty, most airlines offer flight status notifications to their frequent fliers. In these cases, an email is sent, or a phone call is made directly to an affected passenger. Specific, relevant information is sent to a passenger (a process participant) with direct access to menu items to take action.

As in the airport example, a modern, complex business process should be modeled with consideration for how events that affect processes are distributed. Choosing the event pattern is important to understanding the nature of the process and to achieving optimal efficiency. Sometimes an event needs to have guaranteed delivery to one or more participants. This requires a message. Other times, guaranteed delivery will clog up the whole system with alerts, and therefore nothing will get done. In such a case, a broadcast can be used to notify any potentially interested participants. Later in this chapter, we will introduce a pattern that will help you better choose which event type is appropriate.

Chandy and Schulte[1] define the business event as "an event that is meaningful for conducting commercial, industrial, and governmental or trade activities." An event is Boolean in nature, it either happened (True), or, did not (False). More importantly, an event is not only data, but also relevant to a point in time. The event is meaningful because it might affect a business process as an external message or channel, which one or more processes must consume, activate, and respond to.

In Chapters 3, 4, and 5 we described BPMN events. The events we are discussing here are external business events. You can build processes in BPMN that mimic (looping for events and evaluating conditions) the functions of an event processing environment. However, BPMN alone does not fully describe the needed technical capabilities. Nonetheless, we can and will use BPMN to describe event-based processes, which are activated by or respond to the event processing facility.

We call an occurrence of an event an *event instance*. An event instance is uniquely identified by event processing throughout an application or system and acts as a canonical key.

With respect to event process modeling there are two categories of events:

- *External Business Events (EBV's)*—In combination with business rules, these provide channels for messages in BPMN business process. For example, a purchase order has been issued through an X12 EDIFACT file, yet critical equipment has been recalled by the manufacturer, and sensor data has reached a limit.

- *Internal Business Events (IBV's)*—These can arise from the IT infrastructure and BPMN is particularly adept at handling these.

IBE's and EBE's form the global cloud of events. They can be seen indirectly in the OMG's Business Motivation Model which we briefly described in the introduction to this book. Referring to Figure 1–1 of the introduction, IBE's and EBE's emerge from the influencers' portion of the model. Internal influencers can be assessed to be strengths or weaknesses and an internal event such as reaching or missing a key performance indicator can be one of these. External influencers (which are counted as both opportunities and threats) are analyzed as parts of the business plan. The external events we mentioned above (critical equipment recalled, sensor data limit reached) might be influencers.

An assessment is a judgment about some type of influencer. An influencer becomes active when the enterprise decides how to respond to it. The business process or business rules that react to or process the event is connected to an assessment of the event, and to the conjunction of the means and ends of the model.

---

1. Chandy, K. Mani, and W. Roy Schulte. *Event Processing: Designing IT Systems for Agile Companies*. McGraw-Hill Osborne Media, 2009.

An event producer (or source) produces events. Event producers can be as broad as financial market indexes or government economic indicators, or they can be as small as a temperature sensor. Event producers are often a combination of many individual producers. Additionally, business event producers can be external to the organization. Their origins are broad ranging and random. A targeted, external event producer might, for example, be a trading partner's application, service, or business process. In the internet of things, the producer can be a detector, a sensor, or a social networking or email application.

With an event processing method, raw EBV's are recognized at the source. Upon sensing an event, business rules must apply a series of steps that lead to outcomes. Rules can also evaluate conditions against broader event processing patterns or higher orders of logic that correlate current or past events with desired outcomes. Outcomes either control a business process or publish the event. Certainly, capturing and tracking the event for historical purposes is also beneficial.

EVENT ANALYSIS

There are three components to event analysis—identification of:

1. Event producers
2. Event-processing decision logic
3. Event consumers

Analysts should identify the relationships between producers, decision logic, and consumers. In many cases, an event handler is a grid or networked collection of interacting events and you will work across the grid to build up the relationships. In this context, the primary objective of event analysis would be to decide event producers, event characteristics, and the decision logic needed to process the events and deliver the output to the consumers.

A detected event generally moves through a number of phases prior to being placed on an event channel. Part of event analysis is to determine the phases and the controlling logic.

Types of Event Processing

Event processing falls into various levels of complexity. Complex Event Processing (CEP) uses a pattern to identify events. A patterned analysis might span many, possibly millions, of independent conditions and events. Examples of these events might include market abuse, cyber warfare, or changes in trading patterns for market equities. A CEP pattern is a collection of conditions or constraints that indicate the occurrence of an event. CEP patterns might involve many causal, temporal, and spatial dimensions. Despite the complex and rich nature of the information used by CEP, the output is simple: business events that require a response.

As we have already mentioned, not all event processes need CEP. Some processes are singular, or a node on a grid of events. Examples of simple events can be simple business transactions, medical records, or supply-chain transactions processing. Usually the transactions within a process are related, such as a shipping receipt for a purchase order, or a bid for a request for proposal. Ordinary, grid events are filtered, correlated, and routed with little modification other than attribute ornamentation. Correlation might look for related prior events or anticipated future events. As each event happens, the decision logic is applied, and then each event occurrence is routed to the event consumer through a channel. The transformation might then route events. It might merge them with other events, as in a shipment receipt. Then, simple decision logic might translate the events schema into a canonical form. CEP also needs the same type of rule-based event processing.

Event processing can incorporate analytics and intelligent decision management techniques to predict events and mime patterns.

Event Processing and Business Process Models

Business event processing and business process modeling can create an effective combination of timely event pattern detection and dynamic business process execution. Business event processing simplifies the construction of the event-driven business process usage pattern. Event processing identifies and channels business situations (as actionable) and signals the business process to respond. Additionally, even though there are no standards for event processing, many products support graphical, nonprocedural user interfaces that business analysts and managers use to define the event processing interactions and actions.

EVENT MODELING FRAMEWORK (EMF)

As we mentioned in Chapter 1, modern processes are constructed with the three metaphors: business processes, decisions, and events. Each of these metaphors has a perspective, logical components, and a design framework.

The Event Modeling Framework (EMF) develops different components of the event processing systems. It develops and connects the three key event processing concepts:

1. Event-sensing or detecting functions for input events

2. Event decision logic

3. Event channels for consuming processes

The framework is independent of the technologies that process events. Yet all technologies share attributes similar to the ones described here.

The goal of the EMF is to create the fabric of event processing systems and event-driven business processes, and to provide a common framework for specifying event processing solutions and implementations.

Event Decision Logic

In the EMF there are several classes of decisions for event processing which usually occur in the following order:

1.   Detection
2.   Distribution
3.   Aggregation
4.   Correlation
5.   Assignment

Not every event processor includes all of these steps. Also, except for detection, which comes first, it is not required for these steps to be executed in this order. The list shown is ideal, in theory, for all event processing situations:

> **Detection**—In event detection, logic is applied to data monitored by the event detector. A business-relevant event or "event-of-interest" is discovered when the event process matches the logic with the data. For example, perhaps the detected events are equity prices that fall within a specific percentage. For ordinary events, business rules detect the equity that is "of-interest" and whether the percentage falls within the proscribed limit.

> **Distribution**—In event distribution, the detected event is immediately alerted to the affected process or systems according to the logic and levels of participation. As mentioned in Chapter 1, most organizations have four levels of participant involvement: active, passive or monitoring, informational, and uninformed. Detection logic decides the level of involvement and the destination of the distributed event. Distribution logic can be simplistic, as in a burglar alarm during irregular hours. Complex distribution logic might deliver the event based on the scale of the data within the event. For example, a delivery order of a special size for a contract might need a distinct process.

> Events are distributed through two distinct patterns—either through a message or a broadcast. The message corresponds to the BPMN message. Event processing targets the event-activated messages at a process instance. The broadcast distribution method is denoted as a

signal event in BPMN, and is analogous to a radio signal. While a message persists after it is sent, a broadcast is only relevant for a short period of time. An undelivered message might require reattempts to deliver, but unnoticed signal events are simply discarded. Furthermore, messages contain a payload of data, whereas a signal is more likely an event that prompts a participant to retrieve data.

If you use the broadcast and message patterns wisely, it will be easy to optimize process and event models.

Aggregation—Many business events are only meaningful in combination with other events of a similar or related nature. Logical significance might arise from the timing or temporal nature of the other events. In aggregation, event processing uses business rules logic to identify significant events from a group of events. For example, an instance of suspected market abuse might be created by an aggregation of similar trades or trades suspiciously timed. Business rules define the logic of the similarity and the timing.

Correlation—In the introduction, we explained how event processing can play a role in the application-centric usage pattern by detecting internal or external events and correlating these with concurrent processes or data in the enterprise. Active business processes might be identified as intended recipients. For instance, if a vendor fails to certify lab testing during an ongoing testing program administration, a decertification event can raise an exception in a running process. Business rules define what data or process states are included in the correlations and the logic of the match.

Assignment—At the conclusion of the cycle, in assignment, the event is assigned to one or more processes. Business rules can choose which process is assigned to the event for action. As with all rules, the assignment can be as straightforward as the unconditional assignment to a single process, or it can be a time, capability, and dependent assignment.

As shown in Figure 8–4, event processing proceeds in a cyclical fashion until one of the processing steps consumes or replaces another.

Figure 8–4 event processing proceeds until the event is consumed or replaced by another processing step.

BPMN can also describe this type of event processing—for instance, if an event process needs to detect, aggregate, correlate, and assign. The process shown in Figure 8–5 depicts the corresponding BPMN notation.

In this diagram, broadcast events are actively monitored. When a matching signal meets the event criteria (broadcast signal attributes match), the process is triggered. A script is run to match new signal data with what exists in a data

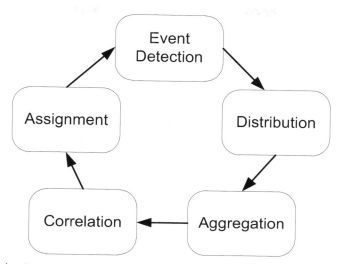

Figure 8–4 *Event interceptor, aggregator, correlator, and assigner.*

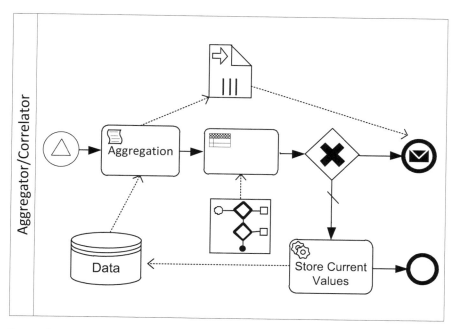

Figure 8–5 *Event detector and distributor.*

source. The rule set determines the action to take (such as data assignment) or if any participants should directly receive the event. The current state (moving average, status, standard deviation, etc.) is updated as a service task.

EVENT CHANNEL

An event channel publishes, signals, or posts events and streams of events as process instances. Traditionally, event processing is complete once the event has been directed to a channel. In more advanced approaches, as shown on Figure 8–4, the event might continue to be processed.

In the assignment or distribution steps, the event channel might transmit multiple events from different event processes. Alternately, it might combine events from many processes. Event decision logic should handle ordering among the events from different processes to create the combined set of events. Again, the looping nature of event processing creates the order of events.

Within BPMN two active shapes respond to event channels: the message and the signal. There are three event cycle phase shapes (summarized in Table 8–1). In an event processing step, the logic conditions detect, aggregate, and correlate are depicted as one condition.

Figure 8–6 shows a BPMN model of a detector and distributor. A condition is detected, resulting from multiple events and data states. When detected, a signal is broadcast to any interested participants.

Event Repository

Most event scenarios connect with a previous process instance or related event. For instance, a power outage event in a smart grid might not be meaningful if it has a very short duration. A single outage of less than a second might be considered as a temporary glitch. However, a large number of short power outages, in combination with other events, could have a different meaning, such as a long or perpetual event. This might indicate an eminent equipment failure, or maybe the need to add capacity to the system. For this reason, an important responsibility of an event processing environment is to record the history of the events flowing through for retrospective analysis and processing.

Decision logic, associated with event retention policies, determines the duration and filtering conditions for retained events. The presence and timing of the information in the repository feed the business rules of the detection, aggregation, and correlation states. This logic is integral to the objectives of event processing.

Figure 8–7 depicts some concepts of the events that are placed in the repository. Event logic might need to identify a significant event. The repository records are stored automatically, "under the hood".

Table 8–1   BPMN Shapes That Respond to Event Processing

Event Cycle Phase	Symbol	Participant Involvement	Usage
Distribution		Informational/ Monitoring/ Screening	Broadcast a message continuously. Participants are responsible for actively monitoring broadcast channel. No guaranteed delivery of signal to participant. No persistence of signal.
Detection, Aggregation, Correlation		Not involved/ Passive	Matches business events and data conditions to a process. Aggregates and filters events so that only relevant triggers start/resume the process.
Assignment		Activates a participant	Triggers a participant to start/resume a process. Contains the detailed data or instructions. Relies on external detection and correlation. Intended for a specific, single participant.

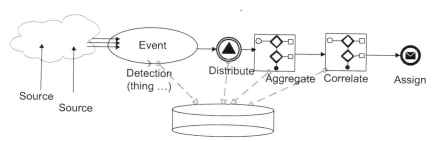

Figure 8–6   *The event repository concept is a critical part of event processing.*

BPMN SHAPES RELEVANT TO EVENT-CENTERED PROCESSES

Business events can start, stop, or interrupt processes. As such, many BPMN shapes can respond to an event-processing channel. Table 8–2 presents these shapes and their uses with business events.

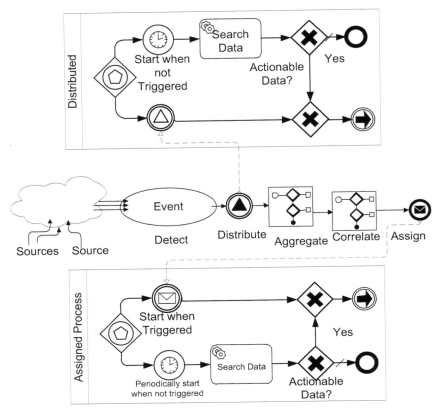

Figure 8–7   *A generic pattern of process response to events.*

BUSINESS EVENTS USAGE PATTERNS

The chapter introduction suggested that there are five basic patterns for business events. In general, these patterns fall within the sequence of event processing and activities shown in Figure 8–6.

Figure 8–7 depicts a process that is distributing an event that is assigned. The event receiver is the connection of the event with the business process. The concepts from the middle of the diagram find events and decide which participants to assign to take action. The qualified business event meets a business process that takes action on those events. As typical practice, the assigned or distributed processes are designed to also look for things to do when no events are received. The timer acts as a backup check to verify that everything is working. For example, on a weekly basis, it may create a report. If anything interesting is found on the report, it may start the process.

Table 8–2   BPMN Shapes Highly Relevant to Event Processing

Shape Category	Shape	Relation to Event Processing
Message Event		As in each of the types in this table, the start, stop, intermediate, and non-interrupting messages are relevant to the business event. Event-based messages are used primarily for point-to-point integration of systems and are usually received by the assignment step in the process.
Signal Event		Used primarily for integration of systems that passively monitors each other's events. These processes use the signal as a condition or side effect. Signals arrive after event detection and distribution.
Condition Event		Used primarily as a monitor of process data. A logical rule or condition will trigger the condition event.
Multi Event		These shapes imply the usage of a channel (distribution or assignment) from an event processor. In the exclusive (pentagon) event, any one of multiple events can trigger the condition. For example, a commodity quote or an economic event will trigger this shape. In an inclusive event, all events must arise.

Opportunistic

Opportunistic is a pattern of combined events that create another event that starts or alters the course of a business process.

In one scenario, a retail company wants to draw a customer into a store with customized offerings. The shopper that is near a store is sent a customized coupon, via SMS, that is specific to their needs.

The high-level event processing steps for this scenario include:

- *Sources*—Opt-in coupon subscribers, wireless carriers, geo-locators.
- *Detect*—When subscriber is within distance, during store hours.
- *Distribute*—Alert customer tracking process that customer is within range.
- *Aggregate*—Customer's shopping behavior with current event.
- *Correlate*—Customer's preferences, identify if there are discounts available that the customer is interested in.
- *Assignment*—Process that generates and transmits the coupon.

The triggered processes include the customer location tracking and coupon generation.

Avoidance

Avoidance is a pattern of events designed for risk management objectives.

One scenario avoids financial and productivity losses that can be caused by the machines that a company owns. When important equipment is recalled or catastrophic defects are noted by news media, equipment managers are notified and mitigating steps are taken.

The high-level event processing steps of avoidance include:

- *Sources*—Manufacturers, vendors of information, news feeds, legal announcements.
- *Detect*—When equipment owned by the company is subject to: bulletins, recalls, lawsuits.
- *Distribute*—Alert equipment manager notification process, Notify operators in the case of urgent recall.
- *Aggregate*—Determine the severity of recall and related recalls for the equipment.
- *Correlate*—Location and status of equipment.
- *Assignment*—Machine health maintenance management according to urgency.

The triggered processes include equipment manager notifications, operator notification, and maintenance management.

Notifying

Notifying is a pattern of events that trigger a flag or a signal that will be observed by a person or a computer system.

One scenario notifies law enforcement when a license plate with a warrant or law enforcement code is detected. Law enforcement agencies use license plate detectors for increase efficiency, effectiveness, and public safety.

The high-level event processing steps include:

- *Sources*—License plate detectors.
- *Detect*—When license plate is subject to investigation.
- *Distribute*—Alert central and local enforcement facilities.
- *Aggregate*—Determine the location of other alerts.
- *Correlate*—Locations and create projection of suspect movement and locations.
- *Assignment*—Case management for probations and law enforcement.

The triggered processes include direct notification of enforcement and case management.

Similar scenarios can be detailed and developed for the deviation and quantitative events types. For instance, market abuse is detected by deviation event types and program trading in derivatives and hedges use the quantitative program types.

SUMMARY

With event-based process modeling, processes become aware—events bring consciousness to the enterprise nervous system. Business events decouple the process from the outside world, yet allow the process to have eyes and ears to comprehend the business environment and respond to changes. The overall result is a more agile business model.

In summary, event processing connects events with decision logic and channels. Decision logic filters, processes, categorizes, and routes sets of one or more events. In the final step, events are delivered to the right process consumers.

In general, event processing proceeds through five stages:

1. Detection
2. Distribution
3. Aggregation
4. Correlation
5. Assignment

Event modeling offers a different view of the enterprise's relationship with its operating environment—the non-process viewpoint. This viewpoint sees the enterprises as a distribution of potential responses to events, states, and outcomes, as opposed to a process model's preconceived map of the sequence of activities.

In the chapters on BPMN, we built up an understanding of process modeling by building up a repertoire of shapes. A number of these shapes, specifically the message, signal, and multi-events, are well-suited to receive the channel output of event processing. When you consider the use of these shapes in different scenarios, you can see that event processing can be used to create highly cooperative processes.

In the requirements chapter, we will provide more details about verbally parsing business events. The approach we advocate in the coming chapters is designed to work directly with a set of basic graphical notations. These empower managers and subject experts. Then process modelers and business decision modelers use these to build the solution.

CHAPTER 9

PROCESS MODELING FRAMEWORK (PMF)

RAPIDLY ALIGNING PROCESSES AND GAINING VISIBILITY USING A STANDARDIZED APPROACH

Successful process modelers use a consistent style that is easy to read and understand. The style should accommodate process improvement and changes without doing violence to the overall structure. In addition to readability and efficiency, an effective process modeling style incorporates the organization's objectives and structure. The modeling style of the Process Modeling Framework (PMF) incorporates these concepts as a guided approach to process discovery and long-term process governance.

Most early process designs were linear, flowing from one person or office machine to the next. They were often batch oriented and isolated from external events and networks. While this type of process is functionally efficient, once established, is difficult to change.

Today's processes must be visible, connected, and agile. Integration with legacy systems is mandatory. Coordination with external events is increasing. Outsourcing, off-shoring, and revitalizing the organization is common practice. Additionally, there are frequent mergers and acquisitions that add and remove processes.

Currently, flowcharting is a widely used practice, yet it is an old way of modeling processes and hardly relevant today. Flowcharting is based on concepts of the early 1900's, well before computers existed. Prior to computer systems, we were buried in paper. Even though nearly everything that can be digitized is, or soon will be, we still find that we do not have timely access to relevant information.

In a large organization, there is a frequent incompatibility between business and technology that contributes to a lack of visibility in end-to-end operations. There is also frequently a lack of alignment among lines of business, as well as between business and IT.

There are many other traditional management principles from the dawn of the industrial revolution that are still highly relevant today. Henri Fayol's views on management (1916) outline division of labor, authority and responsibility, unity of command, unity of direction, scalar chain, and order. These concepts, often used as the basis for modern organizational management, are still widely taught today in business schools. Surprisingly, however, we often find that most of these relevant management principles are often ignored when modeling processes in organizations that practice these management principles.

For instance, we often find an application or technology solution, or, perhaps, an entire process, that solves a short-term tactical problem. Over time, the solution grows "roots". Later, the solution becomes institutionalized and becomes difficult to remove. We therefore find process models that are chaotic and do not reflect the organization that management has worked hard to make. Identifying inefficiencies is a top-down benefit of process discovery, even without process execution. By providing methods that link the modeling efforts to strategy, goals, and objective, the PMF improves the chances that the model will improve alignment and visibility.

Governance, Control, Visibility, and Feedback

As described in the introduction, when using the OMG's Business Maturity Model (BMM), organizations rely on a system of strategic business initiatives from senior managers, who delegate to subordinates to implement the directions. The delegation acts through processes and business rules. However, when a bottom-up process discovery is conducted later, the actual process varies widely from the way management has prescribed business operations to function. Sometimes this is because of legacy process and antiquated technology; sometimes it is due to habit. Sometimes the need to be more efficient created the misaligned processes, as employees used creative on-the-spot (ad-hoc or undocumented) solutions.

We often encounter organizations that spend months (or years) analyzing the daily, manual work of individuals. At the work unit, they might find workers that do not know the business's basic strategy. For example, data entry personnel might copy data into another system from a flat file or printout, but they may not know why. Frequently there is no solution available to solve the technical problem of loading data. Until it becomes documented, standard practice, management might not know of it.

As the business grows and more technology is added, what were two people becomes ten. Eventually, with 20 similar processes, 200 people are doing uniformed, manual labor that soon becomes overwhelming. Communication, even with email, becomes difficult. Management seeks to streamline. Later, when analyzing the process they discover that, according to the workers doing the job, it cannot be done any other way. Clearly, we have 200 people performing a "one-time quick-fix" millions of times before process improvement. Astonishingly, these situations abound in today's paperless, wireless networked economy. This is the cascading effect of a tactical quick-fix decision made with no strategic oversight. To avoid such problems, PMF incorporates a system of governance, control, visibility, and feedback into every process model.

Instead of the bottom-up, follow-the-worker approach to process analysis, the PMF takes a leading role incorporating strategic direction into the process model. Along with the business strategy and objectives, clear measures of success and failure are incorporated.

PMF makes no assumptions that technology will or will not be used. Instead, PMF includes a way to measure the performance of both people and technology. Consequently, the business will always have real data to support any process improvement or the viability of changing strategic direction.

Models that Consider the Organization

According to Jeston and Nelis[1] there are five "gatekeepers" to success in developing process focus and implementing business process management projects across an organization. These gatekeepers can constitute roadblocks to implementing the process. They are:

1. Stakeholders
2. Understanding the magnitude of change
3. The organization's capacity to change
4. Organizational adoption of BPM
5. Technical abilities

These five gatekeepers serve as a measure of the business process maturity that an organization has achieved. The PMF addresses the first two gatekeepers. So, initially, process modeling achieves its best results when division or department leaders are the primary stakeholders of the process. A multi-layered approach to process modeling improves understanding of the magnitude of the change.

Modeling Levels Built on Organizations

At the executive level, division-level processes appear like subprocesses. They show no implementation detail for the objectives. This concept parallels the directives that executives give an organization. Executives' direct reports present a detailed view of the process. They provide a summary to the executives' leadership while providing direction to their subordinates. These subordinates are responsible for getting the actual work done. They generate revenue and directly face customers.

---

1. Jeston and Nelis. Business Process Management, Second Edition: Practical Guidelines to Successful Implementations.

Understanding the magnitude of the change is not always as straightforward as estimating resources and new directives. Process models frequently include interrelated internal and external objectives. By definition, there is no control over external participants. As internal participants are within the organization, we can manage those under our control; meanwhile, we establish cooperative relationships with external participants. For example, consider a bank that makes car loans but does not care about the fine craftsmanship of the automobile. Similarly, the car manufacturer does not care much about the credit score of the buyer. Both sides of this relationship have their own objectives that can change independently of one another, and therefore, should never be in the same diagram. Other examples include:

- Technology that is managed by a centralized IT organization can be beyond control; therefore, it should be considered external. Consuming a shared IT asset requires a flexible interface so that the IT asset and a business process can change independently of each other.

- A car dealership process that orders a custom vehicle does not control the manufacturing process. The dealer simply places an order and assumes the role of a manufacturer's customer. Therefore, the customization of the vehicle is an external process, performed by the manufacturer, and is out of scope. The ordering process and the manufacturer's customization process need to have a flexible interface to allow change without dependencies.

- A process involving business travel via an airline can only include activities related to the objective. Many processes from the airline, security, rental car company, and other participants are involved. Since the travel agency does not control these processes, they are external. Each of these processes has its own life cycle, governed by different organizations.

PMF Overview

The PMF is an effective, structured approach for process modelers. It prescribes how to create accurate process diagrams that reflect a process model. PMF easily models complex process problems without having to "reinvent the wheel" for every diagram. Furthermore, the PMF designs accommodate change management for long-term process. The results include more closely aligned organizational objectives, more visibility, and a more flexible organization prepared to meet changing business conditions.

Through the modeling of many processes in BPMN, common patterns have emerged. These patterns can be applied universally to many situations. In PMF, new process models can be created from just a few templates, regardless of the organization, industry, or process goals. All industries and processes share common usage patterns, and these process templates have been formalized into the core patterns of the PMF.

PMF works well in a wide range of business areas. It has been used to model processes from many different industries including banking, insurance, manufacturing, transportation, and supply chains. PMF can also apply its patterns to common back-office processes such as human resources, purchase orders, help desk, and case management. The approach has been tested in all corners of the world, and has been proven to work for manual processes as well as fully automated processes in software and BPM automation systems.

As opposed to a single, all-inclusive diagram, the multi-tiered modeling approach is an industry standard best practice. Most professionals recommend using two or three layers, based on a subset of BPMN shapes. PMF extends this practice by prescribing both where in the organization hierarchy to layer models, but also where and how to model each process within the layer.

Most process modeling methods also include techniques for monitoring and measuring process goals. Again, PMF takes this best practice a step further by offering a standard template of metrics and indicating when they should be collected.

Change in modern business is an inevitable constant. One method of managing an organization is standardizing or consolidating operations. However, this often leads to inflexible processes. It can also lead to a loss of competitive edge. The new theme in business is agility, visibility, and responsiveness to current events. The PMF ensures that processes can change without interdependency.

Consider how an organization may need to adapt. For example, a process might work well until we add a new line of business or a special promotion. Perhaps, in this case, our sales team made a special deal to win a prestigious client. In general, we avoid unnecessary changes in the way we do business. However, special accommodations must occasionally be made for new process flows and new business rules. Using the traditional, linear flowchart modeling technique, this might require massive changes to many places in a process model. However, with PMF, this new functionality is easily isolated, modularized, and has a minimal impact on existing processes. Importantly, the business objectives remain aligned with those of other organizational divisions.

PMF is an objective-centric method for process design. As shown in Figure 9–1, the process's objective is the central focus. To keep up with dynamics in the business environment, the supporting processes must be adequately agile. The technology that supports objectives must also be flexible. External objectives might include factors such as compliance with laws, regulations, culture, market conditions, or external events such as a drastic change in the stock market or the price of oil. Industry standard best practices are another design objective.

The topics shown in Figure 9–1 are connected by the central, strategic process objective. The content of the outer circles is always changing. Without any changes, we would optimize the process once and never again. Yet, because of

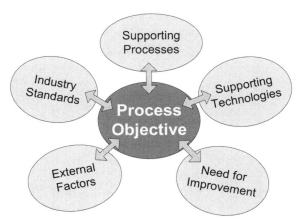

Figure 9–1   *Objective-centric process modeling.*

factors beyond control, we must constantly change and improve the process. Processes, as guided by the central objective, closely align with what is needed now and in the future.

The most valuable aspect of the PMF is its speed in gathering requirements that support the objective. Subject matter experts (SME) tend to disagree on a process because they see it from their own perspectives. This state of disagreement is referred to as "analysis paralysis", and it causes the requirements or process analysis cycle to drag on for weeks. If PMF is used, it can alleviate some of these problems by putting a scope and context to every conversation and by clarifying process objectives.

In modern business, process instances start and end many different ways. Within the process, there might be dozens of variations for lines of business, product types, regions, and other factors. Each variation is likely managed by different people. To handle this, one popular modeling approach is to create one large diagram for each variation. However, each diagram would have to be changed with every change in strategic business direction. Another approach is to create a single, holistic process model for all lines of business, but this creates a model that is difficult to understand and maintain. The PMF combines the best of both approaches. In the PMF, there is a common high-level diagram and modular subprocesses to handle each situation. Each of these subprocesses aligns with business objectives and the organization that governs these objectives.

PMF Structure

The PMF starts with a three-tier model and is designed from the top down. As the process becomes more mature and complex, a five-tier model is typically used. First, let us examine the three-tier model.

As shown in Figure 9–2, a PMF model is defined starting at the top and moving downward.

At the very top, the PMF limits the controller to one strategic business objective, such as processing loan applications, selling goods (order to cash), hiring people (employee on-boarding), or other objectives. The PMF proscribes a controller process that is uncluttered, within one swim lane. PMF models generally do not include direct participant interaction.

On the second level, there is a BPMN diagram for the strategic business objective. An objective can be dissected into various goals. (This is analogous to the organization shown in the Business Motivation Model (BMM) in Figure 1–1, in the introduction.) There are milestones within each of these goals that are in common with all related types of business. The objective diagram defines and guarantees these milestones.

Processes from business unit to business unit vary, and the scenario diagram describes the specific process associated with these variations.

Objective diagrams include some details as limited to goals of the controller diagram. For example, a loan approval scenario never deals with handling money transfers; this must be a separate tactical diagram, aligned under a separate strategic model (controller). Sometimes a loan approval might loop through several iterations of escalation and resubmission for approval. Usually, the objective diagram outlines flow control; therefore, the steps and actions for approval, or persons responsible for these, are defined in a scenario, not in the objective diagram.

Governance and Control

Table 9–1 describes the roles, the governance life cycle, and the contents of each PMF process layer. The top layer enables high-level, strategic continuity on business operations. Governing roles align with the details that are relevant to these levels of management. In this way, the diagrams can adapt to constant change and improvement in business tactics.

The PMF is not only a modeling style, but it also implies a methodology that involves all levels of the organization. Controller diagrams are typically "owned" by senior management. Ownership does not mean they create and maintain the diagram; it means that they manage its life cycle. They are also consumers of the performance and status measurements.

Figure 9–2 and Table 9–1 summarize the first steps for creating a process model with the PMF. First, once the scope of a process has been defined, the roles of the stakeholder can be identified and the appropriate level of modeling can take place. This simplifies the context of the conversations since the objectives of the stakeholder are matched by the detail of the modeling. For instance, directors and senior managers do not want to consider and discuss the details of servicing a business exception.

Next, we use the BPMN modeling tool to describe the process modeling diagrams at each of these levels.

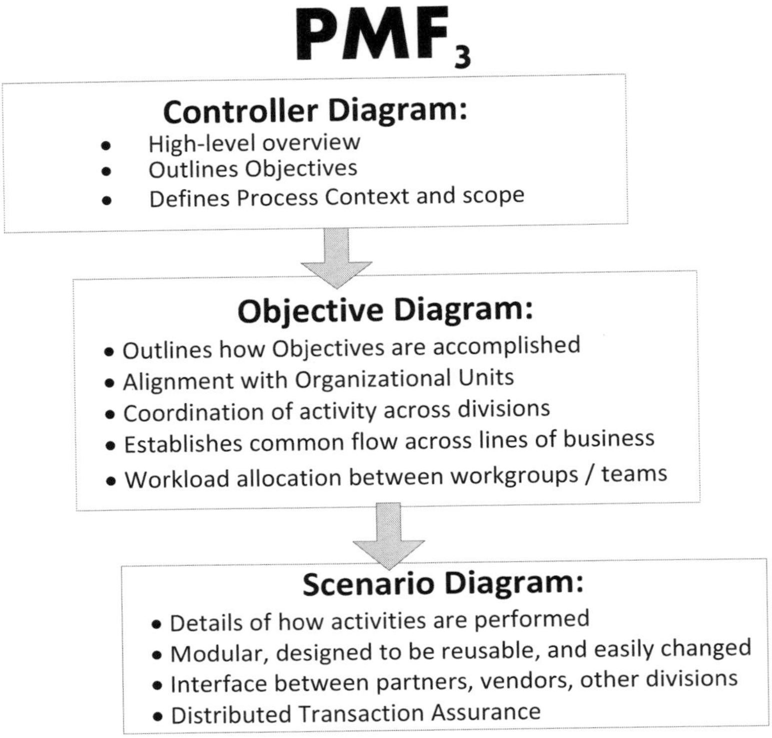

PMF₃

Controller Diagram:
- High-level overview
- Outlines Objectives
- Defines Process Context and scope

Objective Diagram:
- Outlines how Objectives are accomplished
- Alignment with Organizational Units
- Coordination of activity across divisions
- Establishes common flow across lines of business
- Workload allocation between workgroups / teams

Scenario Diagram:
- Details of how activities are performed
- Modular, designed to be reusable, and easily changed
- Interface between partners, vendors, other divisions
- Distributed Transaction Assurance

Figure 9–2   *Process modeling framework, level-3.*

Controller Process

The controller process diagram form explains the process at the highest level. It serves as an executive summary, and provides a scope and context for each of its subprocesses. This objective-based modeling style proscribes the desired outcome from each subprocess. Since it defines a standard set of key performance indicators (KPIs), the approach can be used with virtually any process modeling challenge.

Figure 9–3 shows a typical controller diagram pattern. As a rule of thumb, the controller should contain between two and eight decision points. Once the process instance starts, the controller usually follows a repeating pattern until completion. In general, the controller process should always move forward and never backward. Upstream process flow (or loop-backs) can be used in a lower-level diagram, but rarely in a controller diagram. Instead, use a looping subprocess for each objective. The subprocess is complete and the loop ends when the objective completes. The controller then moves on to the next objective.

Table 9–1   Governance in the PMF

Diagram Level	Governed By	Contains
Controller/ Coordinator	Senior management and strategic business direction.	Flow control, rules, subprocesses. Scope limited to one high-level business objective.
Objective Diagram	Managers, business analysts, and business tactics.	Rules, subprocesses, human and system workflow, exceptional situation handling, internal processing knowledge.
Scenario	Interaction points between internal and external participants or third-party managed technology.	Interaction with external participants, rules, service transactions, transaction assurance.

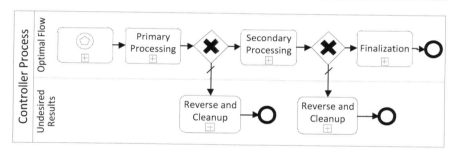

Figure 9–3   *PMF controller diagram.*

The first two tiers of the PMF have only one pool and two lanes. The controller and objective modes use these lanes to describe the processing state. The processing is analogous to a role. However, as the high-level process proceeds, the roles are not within a work-unit such as "Accounting" or "Legal Team". Instead, the roles are more akin to strategic division or modes of operation for underlying business units. For example, activities in an optimal flow achieve a specific role. This is shown in the two lanes of Figure 9–3.

For instance, there is a perspective of a loan origination process from a division-level view. When the loan originates from an external source (reseller, subsidiary, partner, or broker) the applications require exceptional processing to begin the process. After the special origination handler, all following paths are highly similar. Therefore, we put the origination methods in a subprocess, merge the paths, and move forward as only one normal flow. Errors such as bad data, missing required data, etc. should be handled during initialization. This way we incur lower costs later for error correction. The controller would track these errors as KPI's.

As a departure from workflow, people and systems are absent in the first two layers of PMF. Since high-level processes are meaningful outlines of the process, the PMF modeling style is a more understandable diagram to a wider audience. This approach also simplifies changes without affecting major sections of a diagram. PMF follows the management principles of division of labor, authority and responsibility, unity of command, unity of direction, and scalar chains. Therefore, with rigorous modeling at the right level, the PMF adapts to large organizations. For example, it associates accounting processes with accounting and never mixes them with human resources or legal processes.

There is a decision after every subprocess in the controller. Each decision determines whether or not the process should continue, or cleanly exit. This pattern presents unfavorable activity as less than optimal flow. When the process instance encounters an undesired result, the controller process routes the flow to the subprocess "clean exit". For example, the process might reject a credit card application, which requires a series of regulatory compliance processes. However, we do not want to clutter the main diagram with every aspect of regulatory compliance, as laws change frequently, even though regulatory requirements do not. A better solution places the flow of regulatory compliance in another subprocess, preferably in its own diagram. This way you can easily accommodate regulatory changes without affecting the business model. Furthermore, with this approach it is much easier to manage metrics and business rules that govern the subprocesses.

To understand why there is a decision after every subprocess of the controller diagram, examine the following "primary processing" objective diagram (Figure 9–4).

Each phase subprocess from the master diagram elaborates on the objective completion at the needed level of detail and complexity. The completed subprocess instance returns one of these directives: continue, exit, or further processing needed. In the loan approval example, the directive might be approve or reject. Other processes might use success or failed as the result.

Separation of Concerns

One of the basic design principles of an OMG business motivation model is the separation of concerns. This refers to a distinction between ends and means—what we want to do as opposed to what is decided to do. Separation of concerns allows us to distinguish between the objectives of the processes at the objective and scenario level. For example, the subprocess can be changed without changing the objective.

The process in Figure 9–4 does not notify the customer or indicate where to get a credit report. This is a regulatory compliance objective. Since Governance, Risk, and Compliance (GRC) activities have different objectives than loan approvals, they are not included in this subprocess. Instead, another objective process handles GRC; this process has its own set of measurements of time, cost, and success or failure rate.

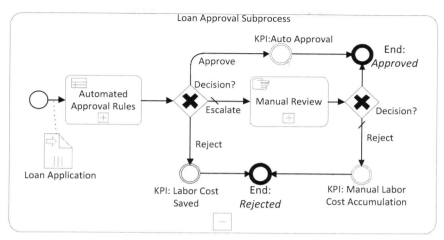

Figure 9–4   *An objective diagram example.*

The separation of concerns idea is analogous to compensation flow in BPMN. A loan processing company is in the business of making loans. Loan rejection is not the optimal result, but because of risks, only good loans are made. It is normal practice to reject loans, and subsequent activity of a rejected loan application is not an exceptional flow. Exceptional flow in BPMN usually refers to process conditions that are not normal. Since loan rejection happens at least as often as loan approval, both paths are normal flow. It is good practice to clearly describe in BPMN where strategic process objectives exist; therefore, only normal flow is used in the controller diagram for both the optimal goal of approving loans and the secondary goal of not approving potentially bad loans. Do not use exceptional flow in a controller diagram. Instead, show exceptions being resolved in lower levels of the PMF.

KPI's: The Metrics of Visibility

As mentioned throughout this book, a large organization's biggest challenge is visibility. In order to achieve this, the PMF defines a standard set of visibility-based reporting metrics and attributes. These reporting metrics and attributes should be computed for every process, without exception. Failure to incorporate measurements of success or failure not only decreases visibility, but also limits subsequent process changes.

According to David Parmenter[1], "A Key Performance Indicator is a set of measures that focus on aspects of the organizational performance that are most critical for the current and future success."

---

1. Parmenter, David. Key Performance Indicators: Developing, Implementing, and Using Winning KPIs.

KPI's are computed at the controller diagram level. The PMF proscribes a standard set of measures that can compute the indicator. A KPI is computed by process-specific measures, such as employee counts, order dollars, or shipment quantities, as factored into the basic measures of the process.

In addition, standard controller measures track the status of the process and determine if the process objectives are completed in alignment with objectives and goals. For example, consider a service level agreement of two days that must be met. Without a start time, due date, and completion time, we would not be able to follow this metric over time.

The basic metrics and attributes in the controller process diagram are straightforward and can be applied to any process.

Basic Measures:

- Process Start Date/Time

- Actual Completion Date/Time

- Expected Completion Date/Time (Due)

Basic Attributes:

- Process Status

- Processing Phase

- Process Instance ID—a unique identifier for the current process instance. A sequential number is sufficient

- Process Instance Name—a name for the process instance, such as "Credit Card Application" or "Computer Purchase"

- Business Instance ID—a unique identifier associated with the primary data type: for example, Customer ID, Order ID, or Purchase Order ID

In Table 9–2, various process types can be included in the same view. This is simple because the terms used are common to all processes and the collective attributes can be applied to any process. For example, in a work order process, "Process Started" is an alias for "Work Order Created Date", and "Process Complete" is an alias for "Job Completion Time". Also in Table 9–2, "Status" describes the action taking place, while the "Regarding" column describes the purpose of the process. For example, in the PO #554 instance we can clearly see that the purchase order is for customer ABC Inc. In the phase column, we can see the name of the subprocess where the flow is currently activated. Then, we refer to the process diagram and determine what is happening in relation to the other activities.

Table 9–2   Standard Metrics and Attribute Data from the Controller Template

Instance	Regarding	Status	Phase	Started	Due	Finished
PO # 554	ABC Inc.	Active	Secondary Processing	Jul 10 9:45 AM	Jul 15 4:00 PM	—
PO # 553	XYZ Company	Finished	End	Jul 9 3:22 PM	Jul 12 4:00 PM	Jul 11 4:52 PM
Work Order #38	John Doe	Active Overdue	Tech Dispatched	Jul 8 4:19 PM	Jul 10 5:00 PM	—

Objective Diagram

Frequently, middle management governs the processes modeled on the objective diagram. Strategic directives from senior management prompt middle management to control and oversee operations. In other words, we execute the strategic business objective (ends). Every strategy has established milestones or process-level goals, that when reached, mean the end of the objective. The objective diagram provides the scope and context of these milestones.

The controller process is notified when a target has been completed, or cannot be completed. It is the responsibility of the controller process to know whether it is better to continue the original plan or reduce losses and terminate. The objective diagram reports the result but does not make the final decision. Also, the objective diagram does not define how to cut losses and reverse course. Instead, a separate objective diagram can define this.

Different processing techniques are required for variations of the process strategy. For example, a loans approval process has several variations of automotive, home, credit card, and other types of processes. Each variation of the loans process has common goals of initialization, approval, regulatory compliance, and funds disbursement. The way each loan type is handled for each of these goals is quite different, but loan type can be processed in a common way.

The objective diagram groups common activity into a common flow. We can describe these common groups of activities as goals. A tactic is defined as a plan for attaining a particular goal. One tactic is employed for certain situations, but another tactic might be used when the environment changes. The objective diagram defines which tactic is used and when.

Each subprocess of a controller diagram (objective) includes its own set of attributes and measures, in addition to the process-level metrics described above. Subprocess Common Attributes and Measures:

- Activity Category
- Activity Status (Active, Suspended, Completed, Skipped, etc.)
- Activity Start Date/Time

- • Activity Due Date/Time
- • Activity Finished Date/Time
- • Iteration Number (for subprocesses that repeat or redo)
- • Result (Success, Cancelled, Error, Redo, Finished, etc.)

One way to compare one like process to another is to generalize the types of activities. The "Activity Category" attribute identifies the types of activities that occur. For example, suppose there are 10,000 instances of customer call-backs for only 3,500 process instances. Since the call-back is a problem resolution, this clearly shows that we have a problem getting things done right the first time.

The "Activity Category" attribute can also aggregate different processes. Often the enterprise will have scores of similar processes. The name of each step might be different, as well as the name of each process. For example, a loans process has 20 variations for different loan types. We might have activity categories of application intake, credit worthiness, account review, funds disbursement, and customer conversion. By aggregating these processes, we can gather statistics on where we are spending our time and money. This information is useful for process improvement.

"Iteration Number" counts a repeating subprocess. The iteration number increases with each repetition. This might be the version number of a contract revision, or it might be the number of times it takes to get a purchase order approved.

The "Result Attribute" provides feedback to the parent (controller) process or the subsequent downstream subprocesses. A contract approval process might have a result of "Approve", "Reject", "Revise", or "Cancel". The result serves as both status information and a recommendation for other participants to follow. For example, the controller process sees a result of "Reject" and takes the path of sub-optimal flow, rather than the perfect path.

In addition to the suggested common measures and attributes for the controller processes, a business objective might have dozens of other performance and status measures. However, only the generic KPIs will be universal and easily understood by a wider audience.

External participants are beyond the control of internal processes. They are also outside the visibility of the internal process, but often are needed for status or performance metrics. This is another reason for using a set of common attributes and measures. For example, banks consume information from credit reporting agencies, and the agencies cannot get their information without the banks reporting payment histories. Both organizations are external to each other. Both are locked in an efficient, symbiotic relationship. Methods for collecting and reporting data vary considerably from one bank to another. Therefore, a common form must be established to accommodate all banks.

The likely outcome of a successful implementation of PMF is a hierarchical structure of process models, similar to Figure 9–5.

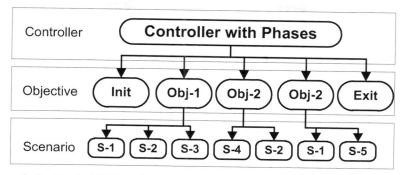

Figure 9–5   *Typical PMF-3 diagram structure for medium size processes.*

Figure 9–5 illustrates a typical hierarchical model for PMF-3. Each rectangle shape in Figure 9–5 represents a diagram, which is a subprocess in its parent diagram. Notice that each objective diagram is only used once, but each tactic may be used many times.

Scenario Diagram

The scenario diagram is less restrictive than the diagrams from the higher layers of the PMF. Processes modeled in a scenario diagram are unique to the organization. There are fewer restrictions on how the scenario diagrams are structured provided they only detail one (and only one) goal of the objective diagram.

Scenario Goals

The scenario diagram can achieve different goals. These goals are, essentially, the reason that a process scenario exists. The goals are explicit or instance specific; perhaps they deliver a product, provide some benefit to a patient, or manage a research budget. These specific goals are tied to the completion of the process.

Martin Ould[1] noted that there are two types of goals that are associated with a business process: point-wise goals and steady state goals. Point-wise goals are the end of the process with respect to a user, customer, or stakeholder. These are the goals of the scenario. Additionally, point-wise goals are related to the individual instance of the process which serves a customer and creates some value for the company in some way.

Alternatively, steady-state goals (process goals) are more like continuous metric objectives: quantified and measurable. The objective and controller levels define these. Examples are a goal for probability of default on any large-scale loan portfolio as .01 or .08, or that month-over-month sales goals exceed a certain predetermined amount or target.

---

1. Ould, Martin. Business Process Management: A Rigorous Approach. 2005.

Achieving the Objectives

A scenario describes the processing steps of an objective. It can also be described as the tactical solution for a business problem. This is the best place to clarify the interactions between participants. The scenario diagram can contain many pools and multiple lanes. There are a few PMF rules about what is in a scenario. All activity should support an objective of the parent activity. Processes typically end in a limited number of states, such as success, fail, or escalate. Figure 9–6 shows an example.

Figure 9–6 shows a hypothetical approval scenario. The process requires multiple input data artifacts. These artifacts would be passed down from the objective diagram, the starting point. In the scenario, management reviews the data and decides the outcome. It might be a revision (a human task) or a system update (a system/service task).

When the service task fails, the data must be fixed manually before attempting another approval. The signal, on the exception flow of the service task, broadcasts the incidence of an error. Affected processes are also notified automatically. Since the signal throw is not necessarily intended for this process, there is no explicit catch for the signal. It could be caught by any process with an intermediate error event handler.

The repair activity has a timer event that is non-interrupting and throws an escalation event. The catch for this escalation is appropriate in the parent diagram. When a parent subprocess catches the escalation, it should be depicted with a non-interrupting event.

There is no limitation on the size of a scenario diagram; however, we have developed a rule of thumb that will suggest where too many goals and too many scenarios are on a diagram. When there are more than five pools or five lanes, you probably need more objective diagrams and more divisions of scenarios. This concept comes from an organizational management theory. Too many diverse objectives leads to miscommunication, lack of visibility, and over-all inefficiency. A division must have a purpose that aligns to the clear strategic objectives. Processes from the scenario model should follow this principle.

PMF 5-Tier Model

As processes become more complex, organizations (large and small) often break them into smaller pieces. These smaller, more detailed process pieces entail more organizational structure, and the processes follow the organizational model to some degree. The full PMF-5 model is beyond the scope of this book, but we will briefly describe the concept.

In process modeling, the models reference internal and external participants. For example, technology that is managed by a central corporate IT organization it often considered external. In a loan process, evaluations of managements 'ability to execute' are handled by an internal participant.

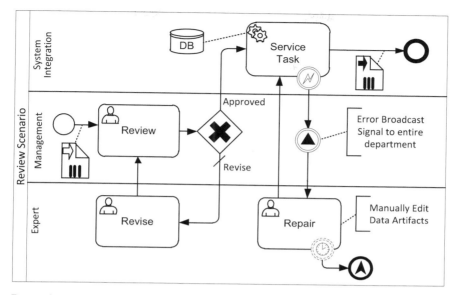

Figure 9–6 *An example scenario diagram showing endings.*

Interactions deal with intersection points, which are points where internal processes interact with external participants. Often, the external process is running, or appears to be running, in parallel. This would imply that both processes are in perfect alignment with business objectives. But in reality objectives shift over time due to external factors on both sides.

Imagine a process diagram for Figure 9–7 if the objectives were modeled in one large, holistic process map. PMF, by methodically analyzing and governing process changes in a large organization, properly divides this model and adds the needed agility.

In the modern world, mass direct communication through email and computer systems obscures the structure of organizations. This is especially true with a large ERP or CRM system. Regardless, organizational structure exists because the business processes exist. One current trend for organizational structure is to create an overlay process that considers processes across the entire organization, not just within one department.

As an organization grows, employee head count also grows, both horizontally and vertically. Increasing numbers of workers are hired (horizontal), which requires more managers (vertical). At some point, managers lead managers who are the source of the organizational chart. Yet what most people do not notice is that the process has grown in the same pattern.

Larger organizations have deeper layers of middle management. More management roles aggregate powerful domains of expertise, but superficial knowledge of how the organization works.

Figure 9–7   *Process intersection example.*

PMF-5 considers the different layers of a large organization. The input and output of one process is treated as a service in another. Thereby, instead of supporting multiple processes in silos with little cross-visibility, all processes have open interfaces. This creates a more modular and more easily reconfigurable organization that management can easily align with market needs, resizing, mergers, and other common business process problems.

As an example of the benefits of open process interfacing, consider a legal team that handles contract approvals for a large corporation. The legal team's customers express concerns about the timeliness of the reviews. But few know what the department does or why it takes so long. Internally, the legal staff is not following corporate policy when creating contracts. Each contract with each customer is made in a one-off fashion. A clear interface to standard process should facilitate hand-offs to Legal for review and changes, and should also serve as a way to monitor the status. The status should be available even when the legal department controls the process. This organization needs feedback within other parts of the organization so that everyone can see the impact of nonstandard processes.

PMF-3 does not require a higher-level model that deals with all contract types, regardless of origin, line of business, consumer verses commercial, etc. This might not be a problem for smaller organizations where a CEO can easily understand many processes. A large enterprise needs more atomic, generic processes. These generic processes produce generic metrics and production numbers. They are easily analyzed for cross-divisional performance and profitability analysis.

General performance metrics and numbers should be available continuously, in real time. Process metrics would be available, in real time, only upon request. Otherwise, the amount of data is overwhelming. PMF-5 helps solve this problem by adding additional layers that match the structure of the business organization.

As shown in Figure 9–8, PMF-5 adds two additional layers to the basic PMF-3 design. The top three layers are similar to PMF-3. The external interface layer is added to provide more agility to both the IT infrastructure and the divisions of the business organization. This allows the implementation of changes without

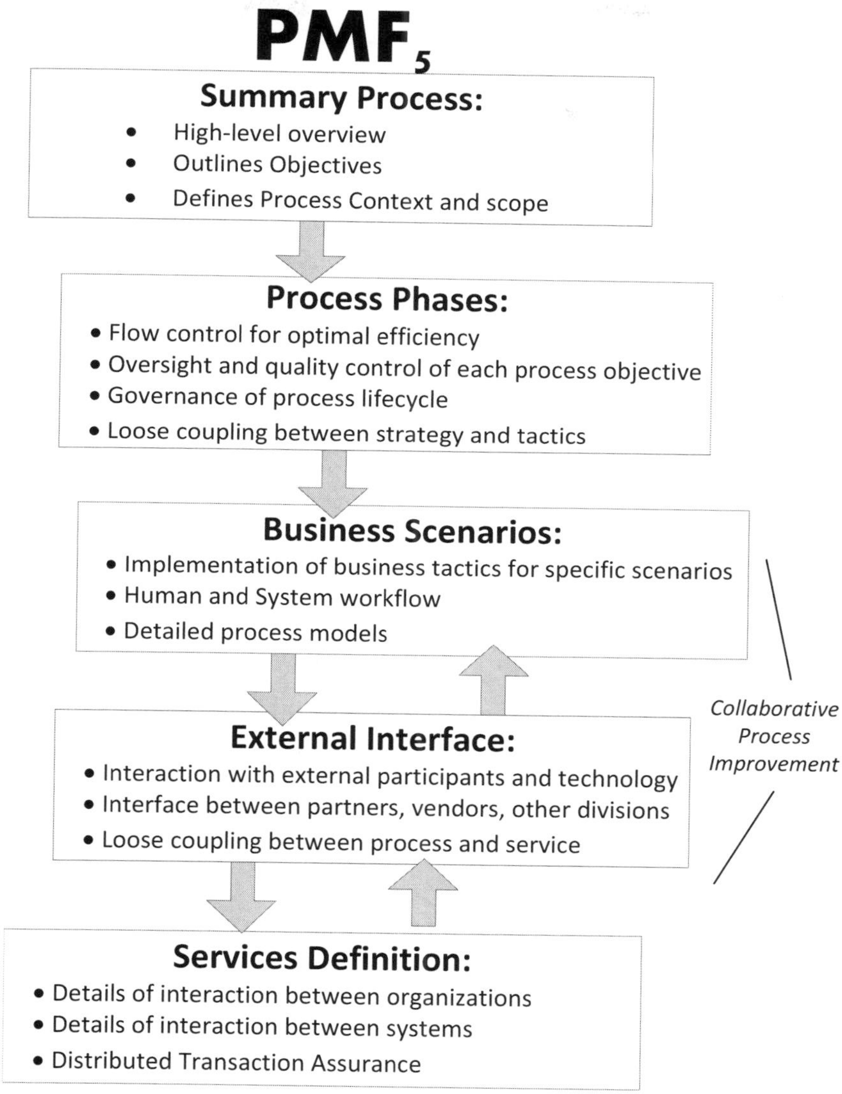

PMF₅

Summary Process:

- High-level overview
- Outlines Objectives
- Defines Process Context and scope

Process Phases:

- Flow control for optimal efficiency
- Oversight and quality control of each process objective
- Governance of process lifecycle
- Loose coupling between strategy and tactics

Business Scenarios:

- Implementation of business tactics for specific scenarios
- Human and System workflow
- Detailed process models

External Interface:

- Interaction with external participants and technology
- Interface between partners, vendors, other divisions
- Loose coupling between process and service

Collaborative Process Improvement

Services Definition:

- Details of interaction between organizations
- Details of interaction between systems
- Distributed Transaction Assurance

Figure 9–8   *Process modeling framework, level-5.*

affecting the process flow. It also allows changes to the process without affecting the services or external organizations.

In PMF-5, processes are kept small, and in the context of one business objective. At a high level (controller or master process), the objective might be more strategic, such as loan application processing. At the lower level (business scenarios), the objective is likely more tactical—for example, how exactly does the business loan get approved? Banks evaluate loans with a probability of default (PD) model. Many factors are prescribed in these models. Subjective factors might include an evaluation of a management quality, business plans, or market conditions. There are objective factors that will be involved. Example factors include metrics such as: loan-to-value and debt service credit ratio.

Now, consider that these PD models for business loan approval are different for each business, country, region, size of loan, etc. There is no one way to model this process on a single diagram. More likely there are dozens of flows for each of these conditions. Much of the decision is based on manual activity, and probably involves multiple systems, and various divisions of the organization.

For more detail on the PMF, please review the material at the publisher's website.

SUMMARY

In this chapter we reviewed a framework for process modeling that works within different levels of the management structure. PMF improves process modeling by creating models that are appropriately detailed.

We have shown that the PMF:

- Creates models that are easy to understand; at the higher levels, the models clearly parallel management objectives.

- Accommodates improvements and optimizations without necessitating wholesale revisions, because the structure of the models parallels the structure of the organization, and process reuse or federation is promoted.

- Easily models complex processes with core patterns and templates.

- Allows process modeling, especially at the higher levels, to proceed at a rapid pace. Once managers have verified the objectives, business analysts and experts can create scenarios that achieve enterprise goals.

- Defines a scope and context to every process discussion.

Moreover, because processes in PMF link to the structure of the organizations, their goals and objectives are directly linked. The PMF provides facilities for:

- Governance: as shown in Table 9–2, the correct detail of the process is assigned to the correct stakeholder.

- Controls: standard attributes and measures simplify the computation of KPI's.

- Visibility: process models are connected to the goals and objectives of the organization.

With PMF, organizations can achieve more complex process scenarios. The process modeling framework (PMF) incorporates process visibility for successive layers of business units, from division levels to work units.

CHAPTER 10

REQUIREMENTS

A BUSINESS ANALYST'S OR PROCESS ARCHITECT'S GUIDE TO NAVIGATING AN ORGANIZATION'S PROCESSES

OMG's BPMN specification explains the notation and provides a few example diagrams. However, many books offer detailed techniques for building BPMN diagrams. Deciding how to convert a process problem to BPMN is still challenging. Understanding the BPMN language is only a small part of meeting the challenges of process discovery. Before analysts specify with BPMN, they must understand macro-views on how the process works. Or, in many cases, they must understand why the process is not working. In this chapter we will discuss some of the techniques that the authors have used successfully to articulate the requirements of the processes of a large organization.

Sometimes a business process is new and created in "green fields", such as a new line of business. Since the modeling teams are not reverse-engineering the process, this is a simple and easy process to draw. It is likely our discovery target is an existing process, although it might not yet be mature.

REQUIREMENTS AND PROCESS DISCOVERY

At a macro-level, how are the processes that are implicitly hidden identified and "discovered"? This can be accomplished through process discovery. We mistakenly assume that companies know how their processes work; in reality, these processes are often tacit. They are in the minds of the participants. In the pre-BPMN era, there was no obligation to have an end-to-end view of those processes, even in the late '90s. Process discovery closed the gap between the first and third wave, and allowed business processes to be studied as ends within themselves.

Laury Verner defines process discovery as the transformation of the organizational knowledge of current business processes from tacit or implicit to explicit[1]. An explicit process model will communicate a structure and detail of business processes in a way that everyone can understand and then make appropriate decisions. This is one goal of BPMN. Discovery, or approaches to process discovery, can be visualized in fundamental ways. These approaches can be mixed and matched according to the needs or the capabilities of the organization.

Process discovery provides needed insight for the journey from an implicit understanding of what the process is to the explicit description of what the process is. Further, it attempts to identify the problems or sources of the problem that motivate the discovery. Discovery does not occur in a vacuum, and it is therefore essential to also assess the organization's nature and way of thinking—the "mind" of the firm. If we think of process discovery as a problem-solving exercise, the outcome should be at least an idea of some as-is process, and a basis for building the to-be process. From the knowledge base generated, we can provide this insight: the work products that we describe represent the knowledge in the visualization work and analytical work processes.

The primary outputs of process discovery are the process space and topology. Rather than a single unit process, the process space can accommodate entire processes such as the process archetypes described in the introduction. To facilitate this understanding, we do not need to collect all the inter-details of a single process. We might be working up-and-down or across a backbone of the single process in order to develop a thorough understanding. As we detailed in the chapter on PMF, the process space should be characterized by a hierarchy; levels of process modeling allow us to decompose that process into lower-levels, or into a series of layers.

After process discovery, we need to know the topology of that process. What are the different activities of the process? What are the branches and decision points? What is the shape of the process? What is the logic for beginning in the sequential flow of the activities, decisions, and joins? What external events will affect the process? This is an objective of BPMN. Moreover, we have detailed the rules modeling approach in Chapter 7, the event modeling approach in Chapter 8, and a modeling framework in Chapter 9.

Once process discovery is complete, the current practice is to move that process into functional, dynamic management. Due to their static nature, shadow processes will not have the digitized detail of actively managed process.

Process Requirements in BPMN

Early in process discovery, it might be important to understand the as-is and to-be aspects of a business process. It can be useful to know when a process requirement is:

---

1. Verner, Laury. "The Challenge of Process Discovery." *BP Trends*. Web Published, 2004.

- Gathering data in a human interaction
- Needing the support of a system
- Understanding what steps are performed in a software application
- Supporting a business decision through rules
- Responding to a business event

The Challenge of Discovering the Organization's Processes

Many domains of knowledge exist, consisting of varying backgrounds and expertise. There is localized knowledge of a process, yet it is difficult to reach group consensus. In reality, few organizations have a complete end-to-end view of even the most critical processes; their knowledge is fragmented process knowledge. There are many localized domains of knowledge. Each subject matter expert (SME) has four degrees of process understanding:

1. *Expert*—directly involved in the daily process operations, influences the process flow, makes decisions, and generates process data; dictates when the process needs to be changed and recommends ways to improve it

2. *Informed*—understands the process, but not in control of it; acts as a participant to someone else's process, contributes data, and possibly collaborates on decisions

3. *Participant*—understands the basic concepts of a process and is only responsible for performing assigned tasks; has only partial visibility into the activity steps and data

4. *Assumptive*—knows just enough about the process to have a casual conversation about it, although may, on occasion, be an active participant in the process

After years of experience process modeling, expert process modelers will develop a healthy skepticism of SME expertise. SME's frequently only know part of the process. Modern business processes are too complex for an individual to understand it thoroughly. Knowledge of the entire business process comes from several sources.

When the process interview is conducted, the modeling team uses these four degrees of process knowledge to evaluate the confidence level in understanding the process. For example, an assumptive or a participant level knowledge about a task might lead us to draw a collapsed subprocess instead of an actual task. Experience says this is a topic for further investigation. Therefore, we might not draw detailed event processing patterns and tasks for single people, based on a confidence level of less than 50%. It is better to "stub it out" by creating a block diagram than it is to assume too much. Assumptions build on assumptions, and lead to incorrect or partially correct (suboptimal) process designs containing fundamental logic flaws.

Processes are suboptimal (and sometimes dysfunctional) due to four major reasons:

1. People do not understand process goals or directives.

2. Legacy systems or processes are no longer relevant or effective.

3. People disagree on what the process should be (pushing their own agenda rather than the greater good of the organization).

4. There is an identity crisis (what is a worker's actual role and value in the organization versus what the organization wants the worker to do) and/or resistance to change.

Traditional process modeling techniques often refer to "as-is" versus "to-be", or "current-state" versus "future state". Often, organizations spend tremendous efforts documenting the as-is process. The process model can quickly become outdated, and few people understand it. This becomes a problem when trying to understand any process.

Typically, process analysis is motivated by the need to improve. The methods of analyzing the current state can be very slow, yet large organizations spend hundreds of hours of work on this. It is inefficient because the result is to promote change. Hundreds of pages of text and diagrams are wasted on analyzing and revisiting the past. Processes do not suddenly change; they slowly evolve over time. Therefore, any analysis effort, lasting more than a few weeks, often creates an inaccurate, out-of-date model. By the time modeling teams have finished analyzing the as-is process, it may have already changed.

There can be considerable value in doing a full as-is process inventory. The level of detail required for understanding what processes exist and how they work should not require months or years of effort. Instead, focus on the following:

- Top-level goals
- Sub-goals
- Metrics for success or failure

Before diving too deep into any one area, move to the next process. Otherwise, the discovery team might get bogged down in endless meetings where details are plentiful, but clear objectives are, at best, sketchy. After understanding the broader range of processes in an organization, it is easier to determine what is of value and what exists to support other processes. In other words, identify what processes support the organization and what parts of the organization exist solely to support processes.

The blank canvas is a common challenge for all process modeling teams. The canvas is where the process is envisioned or drawn. A blank canvas means starting from scratch, with no shapes. Somewhere a process exists, but the problem is discovering what business events and decisions make up the process. Ultimately, process boundaries have an arbitrary nature. The best process models represent the organization's structure, based on relevant business event triggers and subsequent decisions.

To overcome the blank canvas challenge, the following rules serve as a guide for navigating an organization and illustrating its processes:

1. A process is an organization of events that occur in a sequence.

    - A normal sequence consists of expected, desired events.

    - A suboptimal sequence consists of events that might occur that have associated corrective actions to help optimize the efficiency.

    - Abnormal/unexpected events always exist, but you cannot model all of them. These conditions are handled by supervisors, managers, executives, etc, escalating up the organization chart until someone makes a directive decision.

    - Use event modeling techniques (explained in Chapter 8) instead of process sequence when there are few or no clear, organized process milestones.

    - Use business rules modeling (explained in Chapter 7) when there are many logical steps that support a gateway.

2. A process has a scope and a context of events that are relevant to a business motivation.

    - Not all events are business events. Not all business events are relevant process events. Not all activities are relevant process activities. A process is not a process simply because we say it is. It is a sequence of events driven by a business motivation, controlled by decisions (rules), and backed by data.

    - Much like an organization, a process has a hierarchy, often aligning to an organization chart.

    - Higher-level processes consist of little operational activity detail but produce a wealth of visibility data, metrics, KPIs, statistics, etc.

    - Lower-level process models contain the fine-grained details of how work is performed in a given division or department but never show the entire end-to-end process.

    - It is not efficient to create a huge single process model because it will not be maintainable, scalable, or sustainable.

3.   A process generates data.

- Data never generates a process. Data does not motivate a process. Rather, data is produced by either business events (unexpected/unorganized), business rules (validated, derived), or business processes (expected/organized).
- A common mistake is to follow the processing of data. Instead, follow the initial business motivators for having the data. Often, data exists because of legacy attempts to automate processes based on outdated technology. Basing a new process model on these assumptions is flawed logic.
- Technology such as computer programs and databases were put in place to support the process. Do not confuse the need for having these systems by creating processes based on the requirements/limitations of these systems. It is likely there were compromises made to the ideal process when these technologies were put in place.

In general, a process should follow a high-level flow. For example, a loans process will involve an application, an approval, underwriting, and disbursement. These high-level steps can be referred to as *process phases.* Other examples include:

- *Contracting*—RFI, RFP, RFQ, Selection, Pilot, Purchase
- *Sales*—Order Receipt, Price Negotiations, Fulfillment, Payment, Follow-Up
- *Machine Health*—Acquisition, Preventive Maintenance, Restoration, Upgrade, Salvage
- *Hiring*—Create Position, Approval, Recruiting, Interviewing, Pre-Hire, On-Boarding
- *General Procurement*—PR, Approval, Vendor Selection, PO, Receiving, Inventory

There are two, seemingly opposing, motivations in process modeling. Organizations have the need to monitor and control a process. They also allow seek enough freedom for operations to empower local decisions. Therefore, the two motivations are:

1.   Employees need to be empowered.
2.   Executives need to have control and visibility.

Process modeling for improvement balances these motivators. Too much empowerment leads to lack of visibility and control. Too much control creates a pernicious bureaucracy where nothing gets done without many approvals.

Workers rarely know where they fit in the overall end-to-end process. The art of process modeling lies in identifying goals, process phases, the organization, the participants, the supporting data, and, finally, the person who does the work.

It is essential to collect and model process phases as early as possible. This will set the context and scope of all discussions. Start from the top down, not the bottom up. Successful process modelers follow the organizational structure. An organization is structured, if not led, from the top down. Therefore, the processes must be designed to operate from the top down, as well. A bottom-up approach is terribly inefficient and does not provide a comprehensive picture of the organization.

When a modeler interviews at the executive level, a high-level process emerges where the strategic business plan is executed (see the BMM, in Chapter 1). Many departments or divisions are involved, and the plan works like a well-oiled machine where everyone follows directives. Executive-level organizations either believe their processes are particularly unique, or they seek solutions to problems that have already been solved by the software industry. In the latter, they seek an "out-of-the-box" product to solve their problems. Either way, the statement says the same thing; the entire business process is simply not understood. Rarely can an executive talk about an insightful "day in the life" of a worker.

Activity workers can discuss their activities in extraordinary detail. This will likely include activities related to the goals, but will also include ad-hoc (tacit) processes learned on the job by observing others. Over time, tools, technologies, and techniques are employed to solve many tactical problems. Performance demands on the workers pressure them to find creative ways to solve problems. When a process does not meet the unit's needs, it is adapted locally, often with disregard to regulations, corporate policy, and process objectives. Many of these quick-fix solutions quickly become part of the organization's culture, and thus part of the process as well. Some adaptations serve the organization well, while others do not.

Frequently, process requirements interviews are tainted by subjective experience. That is, the interview is based on the individual worker's personal experiences, and modeling cannot determine what is normal and what is not. It is also difficult to determine what is supporting a process goal verses what is done to support a legacy technology or tactic. Many inconsistencies exist, and the more people you add to the conversation, the less they all tend to agree.

Frequently, we find undesired, suboptimal processes such as a "swivel chair integration". For example, a worker might say "I enter this into SAP. Then, I enter this into PeopleSoft. Then, after I get an email from Joe Smith I send out a status spreadsheet to my team and generate a report". In reality, few of the steps described by the worker support the business process. They are the tangles of technology, adopted to solve legacy problems. Small, tactical "quick fixes" become part of the process, and over time the rationale is forgotten. Technology is purchased to fix a significant pain-point, but often the full job of automating the process is never finished. Typically, 80% automation is initially adequate. Then, major customizations to the system are made. Most customizations take much longer than expected, and the business needs changes faster than can be provided. This phenomenon creates an environment where hybrid automated and manual processes occur.

Symptoms of Suboptimal Processes

While many different issues can inhibit process efficiency, we have found some common symptoms of inefficient processes. Also, there are straightforward process design solutions that improve efficiency problems.

The symptoms can be detected at various levels in the organization. One can be complaints of overwork. More frequently, we tend to give more weight to the managers' concerns. An overworked employee might suggest that business is at capacity. Otherwise, the process might be inefficient and burdened by redundant, unnecessary tasks. Without consideration of the larger organization, designing low-level improvements might create many adverse affects as well as positive improvements.

Process Solutions for Agility

When organizations seek "process agility", they seek lower-level division or department process change, independent from higher-level directives. Multiple regions are involved; or, with outsourcing, partners, and other exceptional situations, there are many process variations. Market demands can drive repeated process change. For these agility objectives, expect many subprocesses, defined by high-level objectives. The process design objective should leave the implementation details up to the unit-managers, distributed throughout the organization. Instead of rigid, encompassing processes, use multiple smaller subprocesses, governed by division leaders. To ensure compliance with process objectives, connect divisional-level processes to a higher-level governing process.

Process Solutions for Visibility

When organizations seek "process visibility", higher-level division or executive teams desire an understanding of what employees are doing. Some symptoms of lack of visibility include over-analyzing quarterly reports, overuse of spreadsheets, and email. Workers might have in-boxes full of forwarded and copied mail regarding operations decisions. Here, communication becomes the decision bottleneck, no matter what channel (email, phone, chat, etc.). A lack of process context causes the communication deluge. We often find this problem when a large package system is used (such as a CRM or ERP system), but there are many process steps spanning multiple organizational divisions. Business Intelligence (BI) and elaborate reporting rarely solve this problem. Instead, consider structuring the process around the metrics, KPIs, and objectives, and structuring less around the data being produced by the process.

Process Solutions for Standardization

When organizations seek "process standardization", this is because personnel have been trained in an ad-hoc or word-of-mouth basis. Individual performance objectives dominate and there is with less focus on the entire organization. Low-level actions affect the higher-level processes. In other words, a process does not exist. Instead, business events occur, and personnel haphazardly find the events and act on them. For example, an organization might have outgrown its tools: a simplistic home-grown database application, that worked well when the organization was small, has become unstable. Symptoms of this problem include work "falling through the cracks", inconsistent decisions, and quality control issues. In order to fix this, the organization should first establish a high-level process, and then iteratively add subprocesses. The process should include decision-based rules, governed by division leaders. The organization should use decision management and rule-based approaches to monitor what decisions are being made (on most gateway and merge points) and closely monitor deviations from established standards.

Process Solutions for Complexity

When organizations opine, "My process is too complex to model fully," they usually have a highly event-centric environment. A rigid, well-defined process cannot be developed. Often the only possibility is to model the high-level objectives and goals. However, it is possible with event modeling (as explained in Chapter 8) to model the chain of events and rules that assign or correlate the business events to active business processes. This adds process context to highly event-centric environments where previously, only data existed. Eventually, consistent patterns can be found. Over time, with the five types of event rules, a more structured process emerges. A high-level process model might identify areas of automation with rules and areas for process improvement. It also provides an executive summary in which metrics and KPIs are extracted from raw data and shown in a structured process phase model.

The Stakeholder Interview

As the interviewer, you should open an interview with the following statement/question:

> *In general, a process follows a common flow, regardless of what product/service/region/division is involved. There are typically a few steps at a high level that are always in common. There tend to be about four to five relevant steps, including the start, but there can be as many as seven or eight. We call these process phases. What are the phases of your process?*

Then, list the process phases, and question the level of detail of each. Frequently the interviewer hears too many details for the first few iterations of this exercise. Stakeholders often speak of all the conditions and exceptional situations that are not relevant at this level. Instead, these exceptions and conditions exist inside the process phases, not as a top-level activity.

One goal for the top-level diagram is to identify a common ground from which all process variations flow. It is not always possible to fit every line of business into one objective diagram, so if something just does not fit the pattern, consider starting another diagram using the same technique.

The objective is to identify the key checkpoints of the process. A phase is a checkpoint where, after passing through the checkpoint, there is no turning back to a previous state. For example, after a loan has changed from "New" to "Pending Approval" you can never revert back to the "New" state. After a loan has been denied, a decision is made and the state is changed to "Rejected", and eventually the overall process status is "Complete". There is no turning back from these states.

The process phases not only identify the process model, but also start to define a structure for reporting metrics and KPIs. For example, you may need to determine how long it takes to approve a typical loan application. To do so, measure the time between each process phase, and the process design will immediately have this answer. Without process phases, this becomes a very complex exercise that must be performed by data warehousing and business intelligence tools. But with a proper process model (as mentioned in Chapter 10) this analysis is virtually automatic.

The process phase sets up a structure for scoping further process discovery. A single goal is used for each phase. For example, receiving applications, regardless of channel (web, phone, email, paper, etc.), are grouped together as one process phase. Approval of loans, regardless of type (car, home, credit card, etc.) is grouped as a second phase. You should never mix objectives between phases. This creates a convoluted process model that cannot be sustained or governed over time.

After the phases have been discovered, the next step in the interview is to start at the beginning and dive deeper into each phase. This will involve SMEs who are in charge of this type of activity. Usually the stakeholders (directors and executives) can define the phases. You should involve different people as the modeling team dives deeper, but avoid meeting with too many stakeholders. Instead, call in the people best qualified to answer questions about the process phases at the time when their expertise is most relevant. Do not include more than three to four people in these interviews. More people mean more opinions. Furthermore, one or two people tend to dominate the conversation, pushing their own agendas, not letting the others speak.

SUMMARY

It is essential to select the category of the process—for example, is it a document-centric process? If so, expect many approvals and revisions. Or, is it more event-centric than process-centric? If so, expect a much looser process flow with many events that interrupt or cause the process to move forward. Watch for the rules-centric process, where many variables and logic steps are used to determine the flow, participants, and/or what subprocesses will be used.

We typically use six factors to determine the process category. These factors are listed in order of consideration:

1. *Organization*—Identify the organizational leadership, the lines of business, and the processes that are aligned to these business units.

2. *Goals, Objectives, and Metrics*—Understand the purpose of the process as well as its measurements for success or failure. This is of high importance.

3. *Events*—Identify what triggers the process to start, pause, resume, and complete. Note how frequently these events occur. Are there hundreds of events? Thousands? Millions? If there is a high volume, determine what event conditions cost the most if not handled efficiently, or what events of opportunity are being missed due to an overwhelming amount of events.

4. *Participant Types*—Identify the participants. Is it a single-person process (series of screen flows) or a multiple-person interaction? Is it a workgroup process, or enterprise-wide? Are the participants solely internal or is there significant interaction with partners, customers, vendors, or other third parties?

5. *Rules*—Identify the complex rules involved in the process. Are there common rules that can be reused? Are the rules for assigning participants to work? Are there rules that help determine the process path based on data conditions?

6. *Data*—Determine the type of data. Is it a database, documents, or a proprietary application? Who ultimately "owns" the data?

Matching a well-designed process with the organization will create sustained value. After all, an organization will not optimally grow without a flawless underlying process. Goals and objectives, followed by events and policies (rules) drive the process. Since an employee can be replaced with systems or an outsourced firm, there is less emphasis placed on participants. Therefore, organization, objectives, and events are more salient along a wide distribution of measures of success criteria and efficiency. Rules should consistently handle events or process activity. Data is handled later because data is always a product of events, rules, and processes. For example, data by itself cannot generate an event unless it is changed. A change to data is driven by an event or a process before it becomes a data change event. Process data can influence decisions, but this is actually a rule based on data. Therefore, rules have a higher priority than data.

Following these six factors will help you to efficiently and consistently navigate the complex organization and its processes.

For high-level phase diagrams, you first outline objectives, goals, and metrics, instead of starting with swim lanes. Identify the division leadership who ultimately governs these process phases. Then, identify the business events that prompt the process. Next, generalize the roles of the process participants and performers, and determine what rules help to assign work to these participants, as well as what rules affect the process flow. Finally, develop the metrics and KPIs into a full set of data needed to make process decisions. All other data can be stored outside the process as a data store (documents, databases, web services, etc.) and governed independently of process.

CHAPTER II

CONCLUSIONS

SUSTAINABLE CHANGE IN A VOLATILE WORLD

Every stakeholder in business would probably agree that change is the biggest driver in our collective portfolios of process modeling challenges. Certainly, all businesses have seen a breathtaking level of change. Among the changes are:

- The world has been on a war footing for a record-breaking period of time. Indeed, many countries, especially the United States, have had troops with the some of the longest deployments in recorded history.

- Global climate change and environmental calamities are among some of our largest political and economic global issues.

- Finally, financial volatility, including the credit crisis, has been another change driver.

All of these factors (security, climate, and financial instability) are somewhat related, not only in and among themselves, but also in systematic, sympathetic ways. They all share a common influence on the enterprise: they affect risk exposure. As stated in the preface, sustainability is predicated on a balanced relationship between productive and adaptable business processes and risk. Risk concerns the expected value of one or more results of one or more future events.

For instance, the risk associated with climate change is important to business. Energy, agriculture, transportation, construction, municipalities, school districts, travel, food processors, retail sales, and real estate are all examples of industries whose operations and profits can be significantly affected by the weather and changing climate patterns. Weather risk is an important aspect of changes in the economy and changes to the enterprise.

Credit risk is another event-driven change factor. Credit risk is the risk of loss due to a debtor's non-payment of a loan or other line of credit. Even broader is the field of energy risk. Energy risk entails all the risks associated with commodity prices, supply, and political risks.

As risks increase, changes affect the economy, and the outcome is all around us. One method of managing risk is standardizing or consolidating operations, but this often leads to inflexible processes and a loss of competitive edge.

There are two aspects to successfully managing risk. First is the need to identify an organization's important risk exposures. Second is the development of managed response to events and conditions that signal changes in the risk exposures.

Rapidly Aligning Processes and Gaining Visibility, Using a Standardized Approach

As described in Chapter 9, to build processes that are risk-responsive, process modelers need a consistent style that is easy to use and produces models that are easy to read and understand. The style should accommodate process improvement and changes without harming the overall structure. As mentioned in Chapter 10, an effective process modeling style incorporates the organization's objectives and structure.

Historically, most early processes were linear, flowing from one human participant to the next. Many other process efforts have been conducted with mixed results. In the modern phase of process modeling, processes will be built that are visible, connected, responsive to events, and agile. In other words, they will be conscious processes.

GAINING PROCESS VISIBILITY CONTROL AND AGILITY

Traditionally, software is designed by gathering software requirements. In this activity, business analysts document the needs and capabilities of a particular product or service. Many organizations differentiate between requirements and design. However, the outcome is the same: detailed specifications. Once these requirement specifications have been prepared, they are transmitted to IT for coding. For success, the specifications must include test plans including unit testing and regression testing. Most legacy application developments create requirement documents that are "thrown over the wall" and most often the developers are off-shore. In large organizations, software maintenance and development is an expensive, tedious, and frustrating process.

More recently the trend has been short development iterations using methodologies such as SCRUM and Agile. These methods involve the business stakeholders during every phase of development. However there tends to be a lack of high-level controlling authority. The strategic direction of the organization is not well represented. Instead, many silo systems and processes are created that often compete with each other, and are usually incompatible. A better system of process management and IT system management is needed. Business requirements for business process management (BPM) in BPMN have three distinct phases:

1. An initial process discovery phase, where processes, decisions, and events are modeled.
2. A cut-over to active management of the process on an appropriate platform that supports collaboration between business and IT. Here, the traditional requirements fall away.
3. The continuous improvement and maturity of the process over time.

This three-step approach to requirements arises from the different historical perspective of BPM. BPM is a widely-discussed management philosophy that has been growing steadily since the 1990s. A properly-designed process reflects how a business executes its activities, and how it renders its business to its customers. Traditional practices of business requirements are only a portion of the design. Over a longer horizon, these ideas will fall away as process changes, and improvements will be dynamically accommodated by the organization—often without requirements artifacts. In Fingar and Smith's *The Third Wave*[1], the definition of the process states that business process is the complete, dynamically-coordinated set of collaborative and transactional activities that deliver value to a customer.

Controller processes, defined at level one of the PMF, are key definitions of what the business does and how fast they do it. Controller processes present the most value to the customer just as they are. Clearly, processes should be managed and continuously controlled. High-performance companies are building agile enterprises that focus on the processes themselves, embracing game-changing technologies that remove the software development life cycle from the critical path of business change and innovation, and put managers in charge of the process. The traditional ideas of business analysis and formal requirements have changed.

Certainly, BPMN enables a powerful requirements-gathering tool and it can be a part of the over-the-wall requirement. Still, the central focus of BPMN (in combination with visual business rules and business event tools) is to support an agile executing environment and promote active, responsive change. The goal of the PMF is to minimize the requirements-gathering phase and promote a platform that supports an active collaboration between business and IT. This means that your business processes should become digitized as soon as it is advantageous. For important processes (and possibly others), the process documentation should be actively managed.

Still, a transition from legacy practices is needed and, by definition, a requirements phase should be performed. The goal of requirements gathering should be to create a proper transition between the requirements phase and the collaboration phase.

---

1. Fingar and Smith. *Business Process Management the Third Wave.*

Process Execution in BPMN

Ultimately, our requirement for a process-based platform should support business processes, business events, and business rules, as defined by an ongoing evolution of the business operations. Often, at some point it becomes pointless to completely document every process, event, and rule with requirements elicitation, particularly when shadow processes are involved.

As mentioned in the introduction, requirements gathering in business process management involve the three business metaphors: business process, business rules, and business events. These metaphors are the mechanisms that drive the system changes and allow systems to accomplish a high level of dynamic interactions. Practically speaking, the environment we describe will need multidisciplinary models. For instance, in business-to-business applications a group will need expertise in X12 transaction types, ERP, and the corresponding implementation models. Some of the expertise will be technical, and some is business account; all is model driven.

Roughly speaking, documenting every one of these, without the assistance of an active process modeling tool, would be equivalent to defining an employee database and then defining the instances of employees in the tables. We know our employee table needs columns of first name, last name, and middle initial. This is a requirement; but is it a requirement that the table hold the records "John A. Smith, Bob H. Jones, and Sally L. Quill"? In other words, we design a container for the rules, process and events, not the instances of the rules, process and events. When the requirements documents reflect too much, they become unnecessarily complicated. The organization gets locked in analysis-paralysis.

In the new worlds of business-IT collaboration, the business process, events, and business rules will be supported and maintained visually and expressed as BPMN. At deeper levels, every exception will be handled. In addition to process, rules, and events, the advanced environment should support lower level categories of the architecture including user interfaces and data elements for business intelligence. This is accomplished by eliminating manual requirement definitions and connecting business-mandated change with collaboration models.

Use Case for Converging Metaphors

To move the environment away from over-the-wall IT directives, organizations will need a centralized and technologically-consistent IT platform for managing and processing multidisciplinary models. This evolving production platform will support the implementation of any number of models and levels of complexity. In such an environment, all logical components (e.g. rules logic, approval workflows, web-based user interfaces) can be flexibly created and maintained in the enhanced BPMN graphical environment.

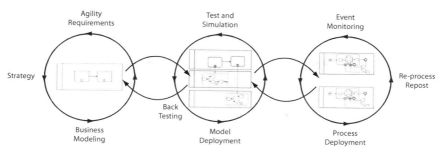

Figure 11–1   *The three tracks of process modeling in BPMN.*

The environment will support disciplined development methods for testing and implementation. Business and IT users create, test, maintain, and deploy new or updated decision models, events, and processes at every phrase. Figure 11–1 depicts the basic model implementation and execution life cycles supported by the enterprise architecture, it also describes the progress of an actively managed process environment.

As models become progressively more detailed, they approach a digitized state. More accurate simulation can be performed and actual testing can be conducted. BPMN creates a graphical modeling environment for implementation and maintenance of all logical components.

To support dynamic change, the platform should provide the following:

- Support for process models of any usage pattern, number, and level of complexity
- Comprehensive mathematical and statistical function library
- The generation of executable code from the graphical models (when necessary)
- Design-time error checking of all process changes and expressions
- Graphical debugging of process steps and business rules
- Regression testing for automated quality assurance of process models
- Tracking, storing, and display of execution statistics

CONCLUSION, THE NEXT PHASE OF PROCESS MODELING

Since the 1930's, business analysts have used flowcharts to describe processes. These largely industrial approaches spawned the workflow diagrams of the 1960's. Legacy flowchart and workflow diagramming approaches are still in widespread use. These techniques focus on mission-level "lines of control" and "areas of responsibility." The origins and outcomes are documentation of "batch-oriented" processes for "command-and-control" management. The systems these techniques spawned, if any, were the stovepipes everyone wished to expel.[1] Since communication networks were limited and manual, these processes were very inwardly focused because the cost of communicating with customers and trading partners was very high. No one would envision a customer creating their own business rules as in modern trading systems or electrical smart grids.

Modeling business processes with BPMN changes the focus from macro-level organization to more atomic objectives or goals. For instance, a process might describe the life cycle of an asset such as a truck or factory robot, rather than describing the mission of the maintenance or manufacturing division.

The focus of legacy flowcharts and workflow diagrams is to define areas of responsibility. Workflows within these diagrams often focus on many objectives. The diagrams do not model a process as a long-running transaction, nor do they assign the process to the participant. Their decision points do not model the perspective of the responsible person, and they make no distinction between business rules and decision gateways. Since there is no distinction between a sequence and a message flow, communication is not specific enough to identify inefficiencies. Without good discovery in a goal-focused way, inefficiencies will be hidden.

BPMN evolved from these and other diagram types, and has some shapes in common, but a BPMN process diagram can show more detail than a flowchart. It documents who performs the tasks, in what order, and in what time frame with activities performed by other participants. Processing steps for multiple process participants can be shown in the same diagram. Communication (interactions) can be plainly documented.

BPMN has now become widely adopted. First, legacy flowchart approaches faded. Then, the process improvements of Six Sigma and Lean broke down barriers by identifying unnecessary activities that move batches of data or work and cede or assume responsibilities. Early BPMN diagrams described process interactions as a large, long-running transaction. Defining these transactions, especially with a Lean mind-set, moves the modeling focus to the process goal and highlights the barriers.

The Next Phase of Process Modeling

Beyond Six Sigma or Lean, event-based architectures and decision modeling are playing an increasingly prominent part of today's advanced process modeling approaches. Organizations use these patterns on a daily basis to interact with and respond to a growing volume of business events and transactions.

To create an effective event-driven, decision-based process, you will need a new kind of analysis. We have covered the salient features of this new analysis in

---

1. A stovepipe is an old computer application that is so tightly bound together that the individual elements upgrade. The stovepipe system must be maintained until it can be entirely replaced.

the chapters on business rules, business events, and the process modeling framework.

Event analysis is an emerging area of business process modeling that develops support for the decision-based processing of enterprise-significant events. It is also increasingly an essential part of strategies for the evolving internet of things, and it is a crucial aspect of modern architectures in High-Consequence Systems Architectures, including C2 applications such as situational awareness.

Consequently, we have two new metaphors that are indispensable in business process modeling: the business event and the business decision.

The outcome is a world that has become process-focused. Since message and transition are critical, legacy flowcharting techniques cannot model the necessary level of complexity. BPMN is a more accurate and theoretically sound modeling tool.

We have shown that BPMN, in combination with these metaphors, does the following important actions:

- Creates models that are easy to understand; at the higher levels, the models clearly parallel management objectives.

- Accommodates improvements and optimizations without necessitating wholesale revisions. Since the structure of the models parallels the structure of the organization, process reuse or federation is promoted.

- Easily models complex processes with core patterns and templates.

- Allows process modeling, especially at the higher levels, to proceed at a rapid pace. Once managers have verified the objectives, business analysts and experts can create scenarios that achieve enterprise goals.

The Integral Process

As technology (particularly BPM technology) progresses, the lines between the business and technical professions merge. In the medical profession, nurses use complex instruments and software and increasingly act more like doctors. In engineering, engineers create their own drawings. In business, business technologists will create their own processes.

This effect is strongest in business. Employees become more self-sufficient and are empowered to create solutions to technical and business problems, with less involvement from IT. This movement started with groupware software and applications such as Access, FoxPro, and spreadsheets. As software designers noted these trends, they created powerful applications such as Microsoft's Share-Point in concert with InfoPath. Another outcome of the progression of technology is the success of BPMN and the many business process suites that support related technologies.

Nonetheless, the widespread adoption of BPMN and other "software-through-pictures" technologies would not have been possible without the rapid evolution of the job skills and technical capabilities of the employee.

In many of today's organizations, the business analyst, manager, or subject matter expert creates and maintains processes and applications. They do this with skills previously considered technical. Their organizations operate in areas where multi-week development cycles would be intolerable. These areas include risk management, fraud detection, and complex areas of finance and investment. To prevent delays, workers make highly technical changes to the applications.

The result of widespread adoption of BPMN and technological advances will not only be more productive businesses, but it will also be more complex, multi-organizational processes. Process areas such as the electrical smart grid and tele-medicine involve many more participants, organizations, activities, events, and decisions.

INDEX